Macmillan/McGraw-Hill READING

Contributors

The Princeton Review, Time Magazine, Accelerated Reader

The Princeton Review is not
affiliated with Princeton
University or ETS.

learning through listening

Students with print disabilities may be eligible to obtain an accessible, audio version
of the pupil edition of this textbook. Please call Recording for the Blind & Dyslexic at
1-800-221-4792 for complete information.

Macmillan/McGraw-Hill

A Division of The **McGraw·Hill** Companies

Published by Macmillan/McGraw-Hill, a division of The McGraw-Hill Companies, Inc., Two Penn Plaza, NY, NY 10121

Printed in the United States of America

ISBN 0-02-188567-2/2, Bk.2
3 4 5 6 7 8 9 110/043 04 03 02

Macmillan/McGraw-Hill READING

Authors

James Flood

Jan E. Hasbrouck

James V. Hoffman

Diane Lapp

Donna Lubcker

Angela Shelf Medearis

Scott Paris

Steven Stahl

Josefina Villamil Tinajero

Karen D. Wood

Macmillan
McGraw-Hill

New York   Farmington

UNIT 1

Look Around

5

UNIT 2

Figure it Out

UNIT 3

STARTING NOW

Look Around

River Winding

Rain falling, what do you grow?
Snow melting, where do you go?
Wind blowing, what trees do you know?
River winding, where do you flow?

by Charlotte Zolotow

The Neighborhood Book

I went to a shop
And bought a good book for Marie.
She took the book
And shook my hand and smiled just for me.
When she was finished reading
She took the book to Paul
Who understood and passed it on
When he had read it all.

Charlie Anderson

by Barbara Abercrombie
illustrated by Mark Graham

*O*ne cold night a cat walked out of the woods, up the steps, across the deck, and into the house where Elizabeth and Sarah lived.

He curled up next to their fireplace to get warm.
He watched the six o'clock news on TV.

He tasted their dinner. He tried out their beds.

He decided to stay, and the girls named him
Charlie. Every morning Charlie disappeared into the
woods again.

At night when he came home, Elizabeth brushed him clean, fed him dinner, and made a space for him at the foot of her bed.

He liked Elizabeth's bed the best. Sometimes she would wake up in the middle of the night and hear him purring in the dark.

Sarah called him Baby and dressed him up in doll clothes.

When it snowed, Elizabeth and Sarah's mother heated Charlie's milk before he left for the woods.

He grew fatter and fatter, and every day he purred louder and louder.

On weekends the girls stayed with their father and stepmother in the city. They wanted to bring Charlie with them, but their mother said he'd miss the woods. "Charlie's a country cat," she told them.

One stormy night Charlie didn't come home. Elizabeth and Sarah stayed out on the deck and called and called his name. But no Charlie.

Where was he? Why wouldn't he come out of the woods? Was he all right?

28

All night long Elizabeth listened to the rain beating on the roof and the wind rattling the windows. Was he cold? Was he hurt? Where was Charlie?

In the morning Elizabeth and Sarah looked for him. They asked the lady down the road if she'd seen their cat. She said no, and offered them cookies. But they were too worried to eat anything, even her chocolate-chip cookies.

They went to the new house on the other side
of the woods. "Have you seen our cat?" they asked.
"His name is Charlie. He's very fat and has gray
striped fur."

"We have a cat with gray striped fur," said the man. "But his name's not Charlie, it's Anderson. He's upstairs, asleep on our bed."

They heard a meow, and down the stairs came a very fat cat with gray striped fur. "Charlie!" Sarah and Elizabeth cried.

"No, that's Anderson," said the woman. "We've had him for seven years. Right, Anderson?"

He looked at her and began to purr.

"But it's *Charlie*," Sarah said.

He looked at her and purred louder.

"Is he ever here at night?" Elizabeth asked.

"Anderson is a hunter," said the man. "He prowls the woods at night."

"Charlie sleeps in my bed at night," Elizabeth said. "He leaves for the woods after breakfast."

"Anderson comes home at breakfast time," said the woman. "He leaves right after dinner." They all looked at the cat. He sat at their feet, very happy and very fat.

They call him Charlie Anderson now.

Sometimes, in bed at night, Elizabeth asks him, "Who do you love best, Charlie Anderson?" And she can hear him purring in the dark.

Just like Elizabeth and Sarah, Charlie has two houses, two beds, two families who love him.

He's a lucky cat.

MEET
Barbara Abercrombie

Barbara Abercrombie writes books for children and adults. She has always enjoyed telling stories. She says, "When I was a little girl, my favorite pastime was making up stories for paper dolls." She likes to act, but writing is most important to her. "I like writing for both children and adults. I find that the stories all come from the same place—trying to make sense of life," she says.

MEET
Mark Graham

Mark Graham was born in Salt Lake City, Utah. He went to New York when he was young to study art. Many people across the United States have seen his paintings in art shows. He has also illustrated several books for children. They include picture books and a biography. When he paints, he tries to use light to make his pictures more interesting. He often uses his three sons as models for his pictures.

Story Questions & Activities

1 What does Charlie do every morning?

2 What do the girls find out about Charlie at the end of the story?

3 Why does Elizabeth ask Charlie whom he loves best?

4 What is this story mostly about?

5 Compare Robbie the Rabbit in "Ann's First Day" to Charlie Anderson. How are these two animals alike? How are they different?

Write a Biography

Elizabeth and Sarah's mother says that Charlie is a "country cat" and wouldn't like the city. Write a biography about Charlie Anderson's life. Explain where he stays at night and where he goes during the day.

Time to Share

Charlie's two families decided to share his time. Make a schedule for Charlie. What time will he wake up in the morning? What time will go to his other house? Does he spend the same number of hours at both houses? Tell what he does and where he is each hour of one whole day.

Make a List

Sarah and Elizabeth's mother says that Charlie would miss the woods if he went to the city. Why do you think a cat might like the woods? Make a list of reasons.

Find Out More

Charlie Anderson has two names. Find out what makes your name special. Is it a kind of flower or a month of the year? Were you named after someone in your family? Can you think of a famous person who has the same name as you?

STUDY SKILLS

Use a Map

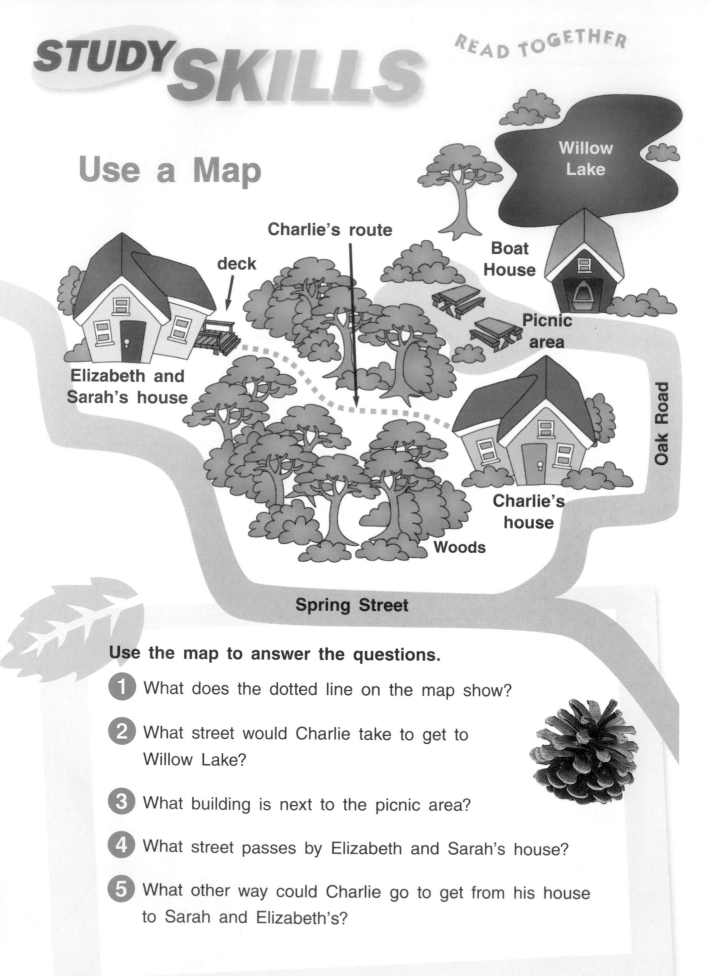

Use the map to answer the questions.

1 What does the dotted line on the map show?

2 What street would Charlie take to get to Willow Lake?

3 What building is next to the picnic area?

4 What street passes by Elizabeth and Sarah's house?

5 What other way could Charlie go to get from his house to Sarah and Elizabeth's?

42

TEST POWER

Reading the story carefully will make the questions easier to answer.

DIRECTIONS:

Read the story. Then read each question about the story.

SAMPLE

The Cloudy Day

"Look," said Andy. "It's cloudy outside."

Pam came to the window. Andy pointed at the clouds. The clouds came and covered up the sun. Soon, it was dark outside. The wind began to blow.

"I think it's going to rain," said Pam. Andy remembered what his mother told him about rain. She said that it was good for the plants. Plants need water to grow.

"That's fine with me," Andy said. He closed all of the windows and doors in the house. Then, he went to the closet and took out a game.

1 What does Andy do when he thinks it will rain?
   ○ Gets upset
   ○ Takes a nap
   ○ Finds something to do inside
   ○ Puts on his raincoat

2 What does Andy remember about the rain?
   ○ That plants need water to grow
   ○ That the cellar will get wet
   ○ That it makes the day longer
   ○ That it rained the week before

My Gifts

Mom gave me two mice
In two wooden cages.
Dad gave me a notebook
With rice paper pages.
The mice race around
In all places and spaces.
Inside my nice new notebook
I draw little mouse faces.

MEET
DOUGLAS KEISTER

Douglas Keister is a photographer and an author. In 1987 he traveled to the rain forest in Central America. He took many photographs of the rain forest and of the people who live there. When he returned home, his friends thought he should use the photographs to write a children's book. *Fernando's Gift* is the result. It is Mr. Keister's first children's book.

FERNANDO'S GIFT
EL REGALO DE FERNANDO

BY DOUGLAS KEISTER

My name is Fernando Vanegas, and I live deep inside the rain forest in Costa Rica. My father, Jubilio, built our house himself. The walls are wood, and the roof is made of tin. At night, the sound of the rain on the roof sings me to sleep.

Before breakfast each morning, while my mother, Cecilia, gives my little sister, Evelyn, her bath, the men in my family gather on the porch and talk. Sometimes my grandfather, Raphael Dias, tells us stories. Even our two dogs seem to listen! I hear that in some other places, they give dogs special names, just like people. We call our dogs Brown Dog and Black Dog.

Mi nombre es Fernando Vanegas y vivo en la parte más profunda de la selva de Costa Rica. Mi papá, Jubilio, construyó nuestra casa solo. Las paredes son de madera y el techo esta hecho de hojalata. Por la noche, el sonido de la lluvia cayendo en el techno me arrulla.

Todas las mañanas antes del desayuno, mientras mi mamá, Cecilia, baña a mi hermanita, Evelyn, los hombres de mi familia se reúnen en el portal y conversan. Hay veces que mi abuelo, Rafael Días, nos cuenta historias. ¡Hasta nuestros dos perros parecen escuchar! He oído que en otros lugares, les dan nombres especiales a los perros, igual que a las personas. A nuestros perros les llamamos Perro Café y Perro Negro.

My father says that he will spend most of the day tending our crop of achiote, a plant that's used to make red dye. Other days, my father spends his time planting trees. He also has a job teaching people about the rain forest.

When it's time for breakfast, my father milks the cow, and my mother and Evelyn chop onions to flavor our meal. This morning we're having rice and beans. If I'm not too full, I might have a banana, too. They grow right outside our house—all I have to do is pick one!

Mi papá dice que se pasará la mayoría del día cuidando nuestra cosecha de achiote, una planta que se usa para hacer tinte rojo. Otros dias, mi papá pasa el tiempo sembrando árboles. Él también trabaja educando a las personas sobre la selva.

A la hora del desayuno, mi papá ordeña la vaca, y mi mamá y Evelyn cortan cebollas para darle sabor a nuestra comida. Esta mañana comeremos arroz y frijoles. Si no estoy muy lleno, puede ser que coma un plátano, también. Ellos crecen afuera de nuestra casa—¡solamente tengo que recoger uno!

After breakfast, I go to school. It's not very far—only about three miles from our house. Often my grandfather and the dogs walk with me. Grandfather knows everything about the rain forest and what to look for along the way: fruits and nuts, insects and lizards, beautiful flowers, maybe even a bright red parrot. This morning he wants to show me a family of squirrel monkeys. They're not easy to find anymore. Grandfather says  that when he was a child, there were many monkeys in the rain forest.

Después del desayuno, me voy a la escuela. No queda muy lejos— solamente unas tres millas de nuestra casa. A menudo mi abuelo y los perros me acompañan. Abuelo sabe todo sobre la selva y lo que se debe buscar en el camino: frutas y nueces, insectos y lagartos, bellas flores, y con suerte un loro rojo brillante. Esta mañana me quiere enseñar una familia de titíes. Ya no son fáciles de encontrar. Abuelo dice que cuando él era niño, había muchos monos en la selva.

Grandfather spots a squirrel monkey at last. He says it's a full-grown adult, even though it's very tiny. Suddenly we hear howler monkeys barking in the treetops above us. The dogs bark right back. The rain forest can be a noisy place sometimes!

Al fin Abuelo encuentra un tití. Dice que es un adulto maduro, aunque es muy pequeño. De pronto oímos unos monos aulladores ladrando en las copas de los árboles encima de nosotros. Los perros les contestan ladrando. ¡Hay veces que la selva es un lugar de mucho ruido!

My school is in the village of Londres. Sometimes our teacher, Mr. Cordova, holds classes outside. Today is a special day at school. It's my friend Carmina's eighth birthday. I want to give her a present, but I haven't decided on one yet.

Mi escuela está en el pueblo de Londres. Hay veces que nuestro maestro, el Sr. Córdova, da las clases al aire libre. Hoy es un día especial en la escuela. Mi amiga Carmina cumple ocho años. Le quiero dar un regalo, pero no he escogido uno todavía.

After school, Carmina and I go fishing. We have a favorite place—a small stream that flows into the big river, Rio Naranjo. On our way to the stream, we see friends from school diving into the cool river waters. We fish for a while, but there are no trout today. We'll have to have something else for supper.

Después de las clases, Carmina y yo vamos a pescar. Tenemos un lugar favorito—un pequeño arroyo que desagua en el río grande, el Río Naranjo. En camino al arroyo, vemos a unos amigos de la escuela saltando al agua fresca del río. Pescamos por un rato, pero hoy no hay truchas. Tendremos que comer otra cosa para la cena.

Carmina wants to show me her favorite climbing tree. It's called a cristobal — and it's a very old one. Carmina's grandfather used to play in it, too, when he was our age. But when we get there, we see that someone has cut the tree down. Who would do such a thing? Maybe my grandfather knows the answer.

Carmina me quiere enseñar su árbol favorito para trepar. Se llama un árbol cristóbal y es muy viejo. El abuelo de Carmina jugaba en él también cuando tenía nuestra edad. Pero cuando llegamos, vemos que alguien lo ha cortado. ¿Quién habrá hecho tal cosa? Quizás mi abuelo sepa.

Grandfather explains that people have been cutting down trees in the rain forest for many years. Often they don't understand the harm they are doing. He tells us that when trees are cut down, animals no longer have a place to live. Trees also help to keep the soil from washing away. Grandfather says that this is why my father's job planting trees and teaching people about the rain forest is so important. Suddenly I know what I will give Carmina for her birthday.

Abuelo nos explica que hace muchos años que la gente corta los árboles en la selva. Con frecuencia ellos no comprenden el daño que hacen. Nos dice que cuando los árboles se cortan, los animales ya no tienen donde vivir. Los árboles también ayudan para que la tierra no se desgaste con el agua. Abuelo dice que por eso el trabajo de mi papá, plantando árboles y educando a las personas sobre la selva, es muy importante. De pronto sé lo que le daré a Carmina para su cumpleaños.

My father has a plant nursery with lots of small cristobal trees in it. If I do some chores for him, he will give me one. That will be Carmina's birthday gift. I decide to let her choose the tree she wants. Then Carmina asks my father if he knows of a place in the rain forest where her tree will be safe.

Mi papá tiene un criadero de plantas con muchos árboles cristóbal. Si hago unas tareas para él, me dará uno. Será el regalo de cumpleaños para Carmina. Decido que ella puede escoger el árbol. Después Carmina le pregunta a mi papá si conoce un lugar en la selva donde estará seguro su árbol.

My father and I know a secret spot deep in the rain forest, near a waterfall. It's a long way, even on horseback. No one else seems to know about it. Carmina's tree should be safe there.

Mi papá y yo sabemos de un lugar secreto en la parte más profunda de la selva, cerca de una cascada. Queda muy lejos, hasta a caballo. Nadie más sabe de este lugar. El árbol de Carmina debe estar seguro allí.

After riding for many miles, we reach our secret spot. Carmina and I plant the little tree together. We make a wish that it will be safe and live a long, long time.

Después de montar a caballo por muchas millas, llegamos a nuestro lugar secreto. Carmina y yo sembramos juntos el arbolito. Deseamos que esté seguro y que viva por mucho, mucho tiempo.

Now, my father and I go to our secret spot whenever we can. Often Carmina comes with us. We may fish or swim or play under the waterfall, but our visits always end with a picnic at Carmina's tree. On our way home, we are happy knowing that it grows tall and strong.

Ahora, mi papá y yo vamos a nuestro lugar secreto cada vez que podemos. Con frecuencia Carmina viene con nosotros. Puede ser que pesquemos, nademos o juguemos debajo de la cascada, pero nuestras visitas siempre terminan con una merienda debajo del árbol de Carmina. En camino a casa, estamos contentos de saber que crece alto y fuerte.

1 Where does this story take place?

2 Why do Carmina and Fernando plant the tree in a secret place?

3 Why is Fernando's gift important?

4 What is this story mostly about?

5 Fernando and Luka's grandmother each give a gift to someone they care about. How are Carmina's and Luka's reactions different?

Write a Magazine Article

Compare the rain forest to a forest near your home, or one that you've visited or learned about. What kind of plants and animals live in each? What do you like about each of them? Make sure to include words that describe.

Give a Gift

When Fernando gives Carmina a tree to plant, he gives her something that also helps the environment. Make up a gift that you could give to a friend that would help the environment, too. Write a paragraph describing your gift and what it would do.

Learn About Costa Rica

Costa Rica is a country in Central America. Find Costa Rica on a map. Draw a picture of the country. Write the name of the ocean to the west of Costa Rica.

Find Out More

Fernando and his family live in the rain forest in Costa Rica. What is the rain forest like? Where else are there rain forests? Why are they important to us?

Read a Chart

Many animals live in rain forests. This **chart** shows several of them. Some of these animals are **endangered**. This means that soon there might not be any more of them.

Rain Forest Wildlife			
Continent	**Animal**	**Food**	**Endangered**
Asia	Orangutan	fruit, figs	yes
	Clouded leopard	monkeys, deer, wild boar	yes
	Flying dragon	ants, termites	no
Africa	Mountain gorilla	leaves, berries, bark	yes
	Cheetah	hares, birds, gazelle	yes
South America	Amazon River dolphin	fish	yes
	Tapir	leaves, bugs, branches	no

Use the chart to answer the questions.

1. What is the chart about?

2. What does the chart tell about each animal?

3. Which animals eat plants?

4. Which of the animals in Asia are endangered?

5. What do rain forests in the three continents have in common?

TEST POWER

Think about how the story's parts fit together.

DIRECTIONS:

Read the story. Then read each question about the story.

SAMPLE

From the Atlantic to the Pacific

The United States is over three thousand miles wide. The land in the east has small hills. The hills are rounded and are not very tall. There are many beaches good for swimming.

The land in the middle of the country is mostly flat. This is where most of the country's crops are grown.

The land in the west has many mountains. They are mostly tall with rough, pointed peaks. On the coast, there are many cliffs. They drop hundreds of feet down into the Pacific Ocean.

Each part of the United States is different from the others. All are beautiful to visit.

1 Which has higher mountains?
   ○ The east
   ○ The west
   ○ The middle of the country
   ○ There are no mountains anywhere.

2 Which conclusion can you draw from this passage?
   ○ The United States has many different kinds of land.
   ○ The land in the east is just like the land in the west.
   ○ Most of the crops are grown in the east.
   ○ There are no good beaches in the east.

City Zoo

At the City Zoo

I saw a paw.

A polar paw on a big white bear.

At the City Zoo

I saw a jaw.

The jaw of a panther sleeping over there.

At the City Zoo

I saw a claw.

The claw of a macaw flying in the air.

Meet Diane Hoyt-Goldsmith

As a little girl growing up in Oregon, Diane Hoyt-Goldsmith loved to read. When she grew up, she went to New York City to study art. Now she lives in California and has written and illustrated many award-winning books about children from different cultures in the United States and around the world.

Meet Cecily Lang

As a teenager in New York City, Cecily Lang liked to draw late at night when everyone else was asleep. She says, "People become artists because they can express the things inside of them that they can't put into words." Ms. Lang cuts and paints layers of paper to make her illustrations. She is the illustrator of several other children's books, including *Pablo's Tree*, by Pat Mora, and *A Birthday Basket for Tía*.

70

The Best Vacation Ever

by Diane Hoyt-Goldsmith
Illustrated by Cecily Lang

February 12, My House, Springfield, Virginia

Dear Josie,

   We're going to drive across the country for our winter vacation! My Aunt is going to stay at our house and take care of Rover. We'll be going to lots of neat places. Too bad we won't be driving through Ohio, but I'll see you this summer. Oops, it's time to leave!

   Your best friend,

   Amanda

   P.S. Guess where we're going first? It's where two men flew the first plane.

Virginia

February 13, Kitty Hawk, North Carolina

Dear Josie,

We're at Kitty Hawk. This morning we went to the museum and learned all about Orville and Wilbur Wright. I like the sand dunes here. Mom and Dad raced us up a sand dune and Mom won! It's too windy and cold to go swimming in the Atlantic Ocean, but Sammy stuck his foot in. He said it felt like ice cubes. He bought a really neat model airplane kit at the museum.

Your best friend,

Amanda

P.S. Tomorrow we're going to drive to the "home of country music."

The Wright brothers tested their airplane at Kitty Hawk because it had high sand dunes and strong winds.

The Wright Brothers Memorial in Kitty Hawk, North Carolina

WILBUR
WRIGHT
ORVILLE
WRIGHT

IN COMMEMORATION OF THE CONQUEST OF THE AIR

ORVILLE

In 1903, Orville Wright flew the first engine-powered airplane. The plane stayed in the air for just 12 seconds. Even so, the brothers showed that their invention worked.

February 15, Nashville, Tennessee

Dear Josie,

Nashville has lots of musicians. We went to the Grand Ole Opry and heard Molly Partridge sing. She wore a white cowboy hat with shiny stones on it.

I think I want to be a country music star when I grow up. I practiced my singing at lunch. Dad said that I might want to think about becoming an astronaut instead. Sammy said that I sounded a little like Rover when he howls.

There are lots of pretty old houses here. You would really like it.

Your country music star friend,

Amanda

P.S. Next we're going to cross the longest river in the U.S.A. Then we're going to visit a place in Texas that you'll never forget.

The Grand Ole Opry,
a famous place to hear
country music.

The Cumberland River
flows through Nashville,
the capital of Tennessee.

The Parthenon is in Centennial Park.
It is an exact model in size and detail of
the Parthenon in Athens, Greece, which
was built in the fifth century B.C.

February 28, San Antonio, Texas

Dear Josie,

Remember the Alamo! This is one place in Texas that nobody ever forgets. There was a big battle here a long time ago. I got a book about a woman who lived through the battle. She must have been really brave.

We had dinner on the River Walk. There are all these restaurants right along a river. Dad had the world's biggest beef burrito. Sammy and I had to help him eat it.

I'm learning some Spanish words here, too. ¡Me encanta éste lugar! (That means this is a really nice place.)

Your amiga,

Amanda

P.S. Guess where we're going? In a few days, we'll be at some of the biggest caves in the world.

The Alamo is the church in an old Spanish mission. In 1836, there was a war between Texas and Mexico. One of the battles took place at the Alamo. A large Mexican army fought against a small group of Texans. The Texans fought for several weeks, but in the end they lost. After more battles, Texas won its independence from Mexico.

The Paseo del Rio, or River Walk, is a popular place to visit. It is 1.2 miles long and 20 feet below the street.

March 2, Carlsbad, New Mexico

Dear Josie,

Did you guess where we were going? We are at Carlsbad Caverns and the caves are huge. It would be kind of scary to walk through them if it were dark, but they have lights the whole way. The caves look like somebody glued diamonds all over them.

Sammy was disappointed because there weren't any bats. The park ranger told us the bats live there in the summer.

We met some kids from Florida. They said that where they live you can sometimes see dolphins playing in the ocean. I want to go there on our next vacation.

Your traveling friend,

Amanda

P.S. Do you know where one of the most famous canyons in the world is? That's where we are going next.

Carlsbad Caverns became a national park in 1930. It is a chain of underground caves. In one of the caves, the ceiling is 285 feet high. That is about half the height of the Washington Monument. An elevator can take visitors down to caves that are 750 and 829 feet underground.

In the summer, millions of bats live in one part of the caverns. When the sun sets, they fly out of the caves in search of insects to eat.

March 5, Grand Canyon, Arizona

Dear Josie,

Guess what? We are at the smallest canyon in the whole world. Just kidding! The Grand Canyon is the largest canyon in the world. I thought the caves were big, but this is huge.

Today we all rode mules down into the Canyon. Sammy fell off right before we got to the bottom. He said he likes riding bikes better than riding mules.

I saw some people on a raft in the Colorado River. They looked really tiny from where we were standing. My dad gave me his binoculars so I could see them better. Mom said maybe we could do that next time.

The park rangers here are really nice. I think that's what I want to be when I'm older.

Your future park ranger friend,

Amanda

P.S. Soon we'll be in a place where people have found animal skeletons that are really old.

The Grand Canyon is the largest canyon in the world. It is 277 miles long. In some places it is 18 miles wide. It is five miles deep. The Colorado River runs through the canyon.

Visitors can travel down into the canyon by walking along trails or by riding mules. As you go down into the canyon, you can see the many layers of the Earth as it was formed.

March 8, Los Angeles, California

Dear Josie,

We made it to La Brea Tar Pits. On the way here, we had a flat tire in San Diego. Mom took Sammy and me for some lunch while Dad fixed the tire. He looked like Sammy did when Sammy fell off the mule.

They have life-size models of the animals that got stuck in the tar pits at La Brea. I feel sorry for all those animals even though Dad told me that it happened a long, long time ago.

We are staying at a hotel on the beach. It's warm here. Mom said that we could go swimming tomorrow. I wonder if there are sharks?

Got to go now, because we are going out to dinner. Then we're going to the Santa Monica Pier. They have a roller coaster there. Hurray!

Your best friend in the world,

Amanda

P.S. The next place we're going is where Rover lives and I live.

Millions of animal skeletons were found at La Brea Tar Pits. These animals lived during the Ice Age. Skeletons of camels, horses, giant bears, giant ground sloths, giant wolves, and sabre-toothed tigers were found. These animals were trapped in the tar when they came to get water to drink. After the animals died, the layers of sticky tar helped to keep their skeletons in good shape for millions of years.

March 10, Springfield, Virginia

Dear Josie,

   We're home! Rover was really glad to see us. He kept jumping up and licking Sammy's face. California was great and we did get to go swimming. I thought I saw a shark, but it was just seaweed. Sammy laughed so hard that he fell down on the beach. Mom said that she had thought it was a shark, too.

   I am making a scrapbook with all the pictures we took. I'll bring it with me when I come to visit. I can't wait for this summer.

   Now, I think I'll be a photographer when I grow up.

Your famous
photographer friend,

Amanda

1 How does Amanda tell her story?

2 Amanda visits Kitty Hawk and Los Angeles. How are these places alike? How are they different?

3 Which place was Amanda's favorite? Tell why you think so.

4 What is this story mostly about?

5 Design a new quarter for one of the states Amanda visits. Which state would you choose? What would you put on the coin?

Write a Travel Guide

Choose two of the places Amanda visited. Write a travel guide that tells about both places. Tell what is the same about both places and what is different. Explain why some people would like the first place better, and others would be more interested in the second place.

Make a Travel Poster

Choose one of the places that Amanda and her family visited. Make a travel poster for it. Show the places Amanda visited and the things she and her family did.

Make a Model

Use clay to make your own model of the Grand Canyon or the Carlsbad Caverns. Look at the pictures in the story for a guide.

Find Out More

Amanda tells Josie that she and her family are going to cross the longest river in the United States. What is that river? How long is it? Which states does it flow through?

Read a Map

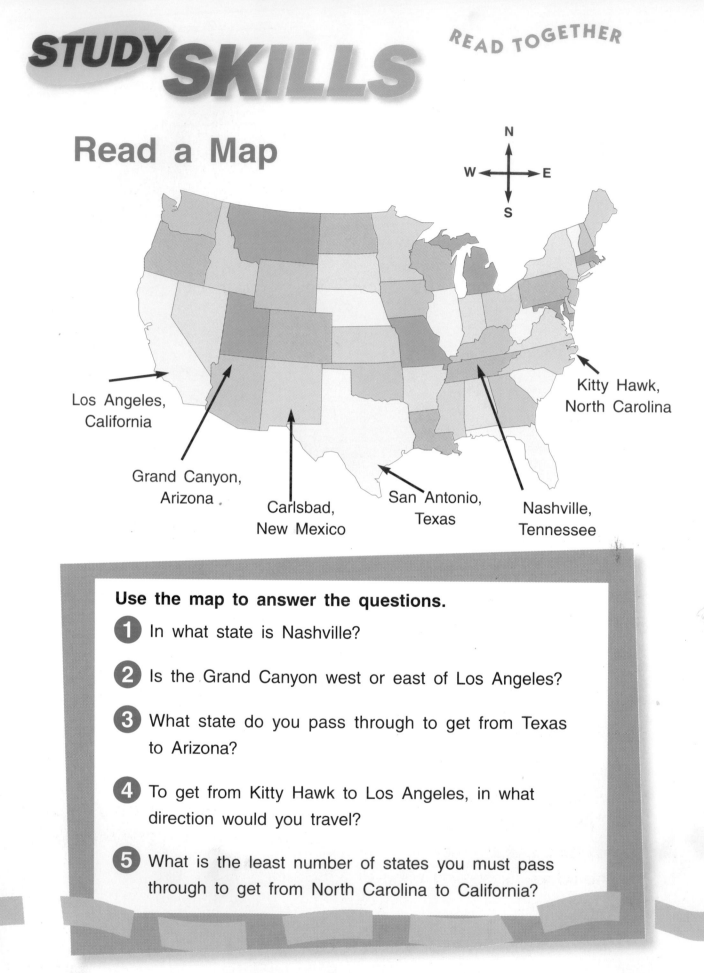

Los Angeles, California

Grand Canyon, Arizona

Carlsbad, New Mexico

San Antonio, Texas

Nashville, Tennessee

Kitty Hawk, North Carolina

Use the map to answer the questions.

1 In what state is Nashville?

2 Is the Grand Canyon west or east of Los Angeles?

3 What state do you pass through to get from Texas to Arizona?

4 To get from Kitty Hawk to Los Angeles, in what direction would you travel?

5 What is the least number of states you must pass through to get from North Carolina to California?

TEST POWER

Read the story again if the questions seem too hard.

DIRECTIONS:
Read the story. Then read each question about the story.

SAMPLE

Dear Diary

I am so excited! Next week Dad and I are going on a plane ride. I have always wanted to fly in a plane. I don't even have to wait until I turn ten after all.

Dad and I have been invited to Uncle Mike's seventieth birthday party. Dad wants me to meet Uncle Mike because I remind him of Uncle Mike. Dad has been saying that since I was born. I am curious to see if I look like Uncle Mike.

We are flying from Kansas City to Montana on Thursday night. We will be back on Sunday. Dad said that he will buy the tickets tomorrow. I will write more then.

1 How is the author different from Uncle Mike?
   ○ The author likes planes.
   ○ The author is not an adult.
   ○ The author likes birthdays.
   ○ Uncle Mike has brown eyes.

2 Which conclusion can you draw from this story?
   ○ The author is looking forward to meeting Uncle Mike.
   ○ The author is happy he is missing school.
   ○ The author is buying the airline tickets tomorrow.
   ○ Uncle Mike is a nice man.

Questions About Bats

How do you photograph a bat at night?
They fly around when there's no light.

And since they sense a lot of tones,
Do they hear the ringing of telephones?

Do all bat ears have perfect pitch?
When bats eat bugs do their throats itch?

When you watch a bat, can the bat see you?
Can you catch a bat with mosquito stew?

Meet Ann Earle

ANN EARLE first became interested in bats when she went on a camping trip out west. Now she often watches them from her backyard in Vermont. She even has two bat houses!

Ms. Earle's book *Zipping, Zapping, Zooming Bats* is a Parent's Choice Award winner.

Meet Henry Cole

HENRY COLE loves to explore the woods and fields around his home in Virginia. There he finds all kinds of bugs and animals to study. Aside from enjoying nature and illustrating children's books, he  teaches science. He also likes to spend time sailing his boat at the seashore.

Mr. Cole has illustrated several books for children, including *Four Famished Foxes and Fosdyke* and *Some Smug Slug.*

Zipping, Zapping, Zooming BATS

by Ann Earle

illustrated by Henry Cole

When the sun goes down, bats come out to hunt.
You have to look quickly to see a bat before it's gone.

Many bats hunt insects. They eat lots of insects.
Each night a bat chomps half its own weight in bugs.
If you weigh 60 pounds, that's like eating 125
peanut-butter-and-jelly sandwiches every day.

Don't be scared if a bat flies past
your head. It won't get into your hair.
It's probably catching a juicy
mosquito.

Bats are terrific hunters. A little brown bat can catch 150 mosquitoes in 15 minutes. The gray bat can gobble 3000 insects in one night.

Bracken Cave in Texas is home to 20 million Mexican free-tailed bats. Together they munch 250 tons of insects every night.

It's a fact that bats help get rid of insects that bite people. Bats also zap moths, beetles, and grasshoppers. These insects eat farmers' crops, the food that you and I need.

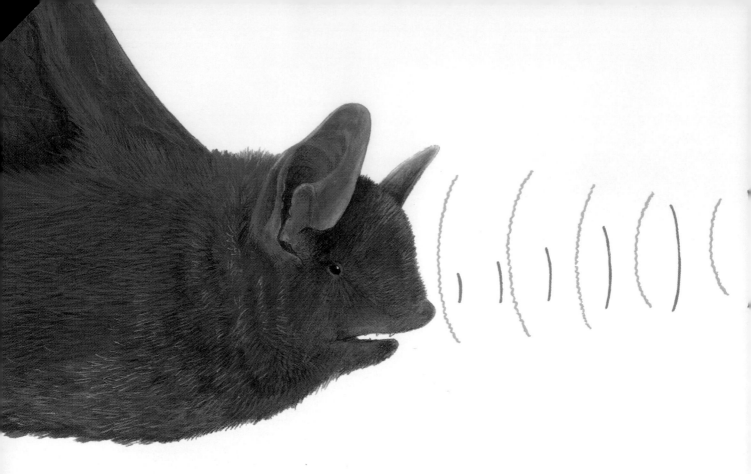

Bats are good hunters because they have a special way of using sound. Bats make high, beeping sounds. These sounds are too high-pitched for our ears, but bat ears can hear things ours can't. The beeps go out from the bat in waves. The sound waves hit objects around the bat. When sound waves hit an object, they bounce back. The bounced sound waves come back to the bat as echoes. The bat can tell by the echoes what kind of insect is near, and exactly where it is. Then the bat can catch it. We call this echolocation.

The echoes that bounce off a tree sound different from the echoes that bounce off a bug. Bats use echolocation to "hear" things that are in their way. They can zoom fast through dark forests and black cave tunnels. If a bat gets into your house, open a door or window. The bat will echolocate, and "hear" the opening it can use to fly out.

Bats are also good hunters because they are expert fliers. Their wings are different from bird wings. Bat wings have long arm bones with extra-long finger bones. A thin skin called a membrane stretches between the bones. The membrane connects the wing bones to the bat's legs and body. It may also join the tail to the legs.

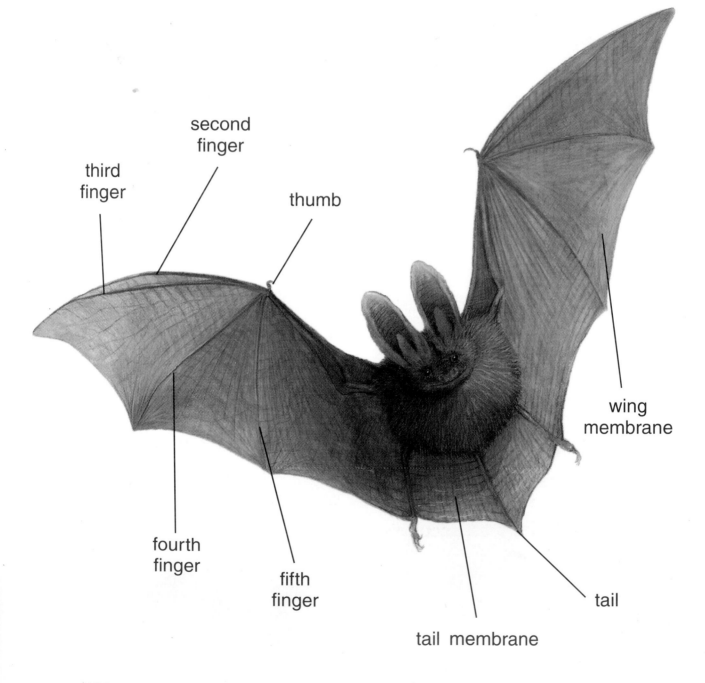

second
finger

third
finger

thumb

wing
membrane

fourth
finger

fifth
finger

tail

tail membrane

Bat wings are like webbed hands. A flying bat can move its wings much the way you can move your fingers. This means a bat can quickly change the shape of its wings. If a bug dodges away, the bat can zigzag fast and chase it. A bat can catch a flying insect in its wing, flip it into its tail membrane, and then scoop it into its mouth.

Bats have hooked claws on their toes and thumbs. When bats sleep or clean themselves, they hang upside down by their toe claws. They use their claws to move around on their roosts, to comb their fur, and to clean their ears. Bats keep themselves as clean as cats, using both their tongues and claws.

Because bats fly at night, many people are scared of them. Sometimes people tell scary stories about vampires that can change into bats. Dracula and other vampires are not real. Bats fly at night because that's when they can find their favorite meals. Bats are really very gentle.

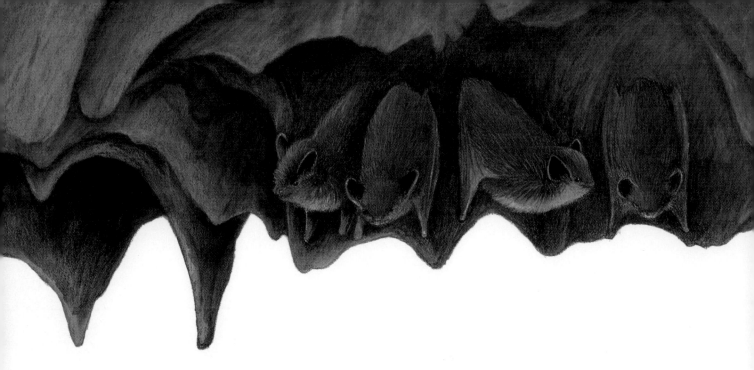

In winter, many bats hibernate. This means the bats sleep deeply. While bats are hibernating, their breathing slows down and their heart rate drops from 900 to 20 beats a minute. Hibernating bats need less energy to stay alive.

Bats get ready for hibernation by stuffing themselves full of food, especially in the last weeks of warm weather. Their bodies store the extra food as fat. This fat will be their food through the winter.

Sometimes when people explore caves, they kill bats by accident. If you went into a cave where bats were hibernating, you would wake them up. Then they would fly to another part of the cave. Each time that happens, the bats use up about a month's supply of fat. If they use up too much stored food, they will starve before spring, when they can hunt again.

If you go into a cave in June or July, be sure to look for baby bats. If you do see pups, never touch or bother them. Leave quickly and quietly.

Bats are mammals. They are the only flying animals that nurse. This means that the mothers' bodies make milk to feed their babies. Bat pups hang together in large groups called nurseries. Each mother returns to feed her pup at least twice a night. The pups need their mothers' milk to survive. If you disturb a nursery cave, the frightened mothers may leave, and the pups will starve.

Besides disturbing their caves, people harm bats by destroying their homes. People close off their attics and tear down old barns. They seal off empty mines and cut down forests, where bats like to live.

Several kinds of bats are now in danger of dying out. In some places there aren't enough bats left to keep down the number of insect pests. Farmers lose crops, and mosquitoes feast on us. People could use poisons to kill bugs, but poisons can be dangerous to humans, other animals, and plants.

There are many ways people can help bats.

Some people put bat houses in their yards. Public parks and nature centers may have houses for large groups of bats.

Groups who care about wild animals are putting gates on cave entrances. Bats can zip easily through gates, but people can't.

In Midfield, Alabama, elementary school children can join the B.A.T. (Bats Are Terrific) club. Members help spread the word that bats are not scary.

If a bat flies past you in the dark, listen closely. Maybe you can hear the soft, fast flutter of its wings before it's gone. Even if you can't, you can be sure that the bat heard you.

111

Story Questions & Activities

1 What time of day do bats hunt?

2 Why is echolocation important for bats?

3 Why do bats live in caves?

4 What is the main idea of this selection?

5 Review the article "Sharks." In what way are both bats and sharks misunderstood creatures?

Write a Report

Compare bats with another kind of animal. How does the animal you chose live? How do they communicate? Do they hunt? Do they sleep all winter? What do they eat? Show what is alike about bats and your animal and what is different.

Make a Bat Flip Book

Use about ten index cards. Draw a bat in the middle of the first card. Continue drawing a bat on each card, making the wings a little bit higher or lower. Staple the cards on one side, making sure to keep them in order. Flip the pages and your bat will appear to zip and zoom!

Bat Math

Some bats eat half their weight in bugs in one night! If a flying fox bat weighed two pounds, how many pounds of bugs would it have to eat to get full?

Find Out More

Bats are animals that are active at night. Find out about another animal that is active at night. Where does it live? What does it eat? How does it find its way in the dark?

Read a Map

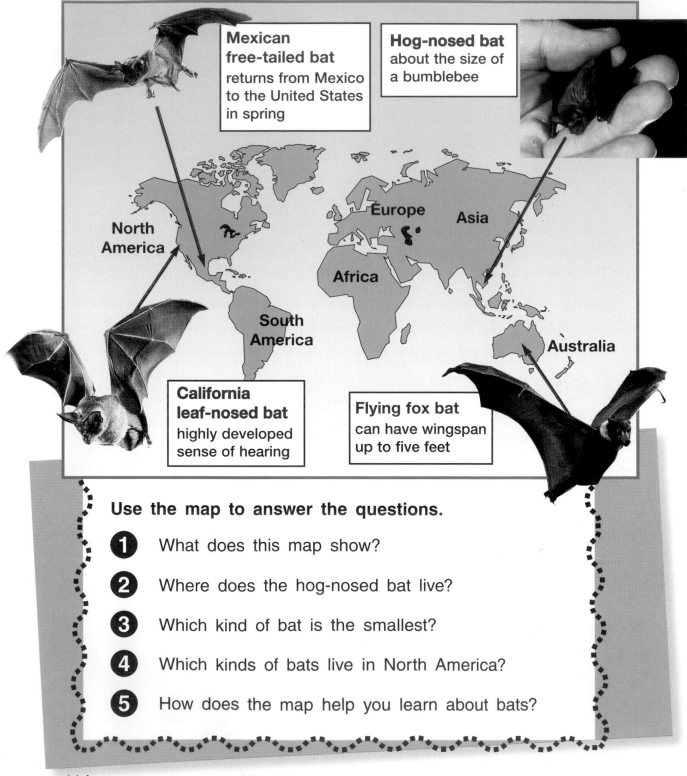

Mexican free-tailed bat returns from Mexico to the United States in spring

Hog-nosed bat about the size of a bumblebee

North America

Europe

Asia

Africa

South America

Australia

California leaf-nosed bat highly developed sense of hearing

Flying fox bat can have wingspan up to five feet

Use the map to answer the questions.

1. What does this map show?

2. Where does the hog-nosed bat live?

3. Which kind of bat is the smallest?

4. Which kinds of bats live in North America?

5. How does the map help you learn about bats?

TEST POWER

Look back in the story for clues if a question is hard for you.

DIRECTIONS:

Read the story. Then read each question about the story.

SAMPLE

The Dinner Guest

John's family was making dinner. They were expecting John's uncle for dinner.

"John, could you please help me?" his mother asked.

John washed the dishes. Then he set the table. He put the forks, knives, and spoons next to the dishes. John was excited to see his uncle. He lived far away in Japan, and John had not seen him for a long time. But John had good memories of his uncle's visits. He always brought something interesting from Japan for John and his sister.

1 John is—
   ○ happy about his uncle's visit
   ○ confused about how to set the table
   ○ ready to go to school
   ○ hungry for dinner

2 Where did John put the forks, knives, and spoons?
   ○ Back in the drawer
   ○ Into the sink
   ○ Into the dishwasher
   ○ Next to the dishes on the table

Good News About Bats

I used to think that bats were awful.
Now I think they're awful nice.
They have been around for ages
And they kind of look like mice.
True, their wings seem sort of phony.
Then again, you must admit:
Bats catch bugs like gnats and beetles,
So they help us quite a bit.

TIME FOR KIDS

These bats live in Asia.

Going BATTY for Bats

Bats Help People! Really!

Who's afraid of the big black bat?
People who don't know how helpful bats can be.

Night falls. Darkness comes. The wind blows leaves around your feet. Suddenly a vampire bat swoops down at you!

Now catch your breath. Scary bat stories have been around for hundreds of years. In real life, bats hardly ever hurt people. The flying mammals are some of nature's biggest helpers.

HOW BATS HELP US

Bats help farmers by eating insects that kill crops. The 20 million Mexican free-tailed bats that live near San Antonio, Texas, eat 250 tons of insects every night! In fact, most bats can eat up to 600 insects in one hour!

COVER AND RIGHT:MERLIN TUTTLE/PHOTO RESEARCHERS

This heart-nosed bat is about to eat an insect.

119

BATS ARE SCARED OF YOU!

Bats should be afraid of people and not the other way around. Today 20 kinds of bats are in danger of dying out. People have burned them out of caves. They have buried them inside mines. "People think every bat is a vampire bat. So they kill all they can find," says Thomas Kunz. He is a scientist who studies bats.

The good news is that some people are working hard to keep bats safe. A group called Bat Conservation International has built iron gates to cover the fronts of some bat caves and mines.

Some people build bat houses in their yards.

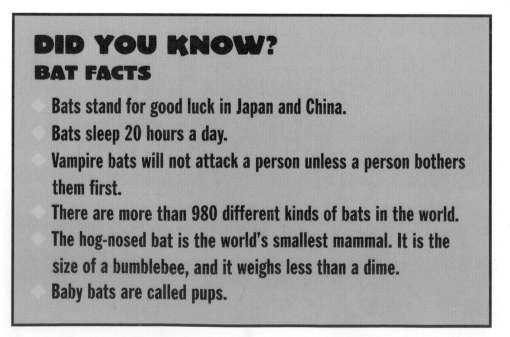

DID YOU KNOW?
BAT FACTS

- Bats stand for good luck in Japan and China.
- Bats sleep 20 hours a day.
- Vampire bats will not attack a person unless a person bothers them first.
- There are more than 980 different kinds of bats in the world.
- The hog-nosed bat is the world's smallest mammal. It is the size of a bumblebee, and it weighs less than a dime.
- Baby bats are called pups.

Many people come to parts of Texas to watch bats fly.

The gates let bats in. But they keep out people who would hurt them. The group is also teaching people about all the good things bats do.

BATS ARE OUR FRIENDS

Some of the bats' best friends live in Austin, Texas. People there are proud of the one million bats that fly out from under the Congress Avenue Bridge when the sun goes down. The bats make up the largest bat colony in any city in the world.

So don't get scared if you happen to see a bat. The scariest things about them are the stories people tell.

FIND OUT MORE
Visit our website:
www.mhschool.com/reading

Based on an article in *TIME FOR KIDS*.

Story Questions & Activities

1 How do bats help farmers?

2 Why should bats be afraid of people?

3 Why do you think that Bat Conservation International is teaching people about all the good things bats do?

4 What is the main idea of this selection?

5 Compare "Going Batty for Bats" to "Zipping, Zapping, Zooming Bats." What facts are the same? Which ones are different?

Write a Speech

Write a speech that will help people be less afraid of bats. Give reasons why people are scared of bats. Compare these reasons to facts about bats. Explain how bats help people.

Make an Advertisement

Think of another animal that seems scary but really isn't. Create an ad for this animal. Give facts about the animal. Explain why people should not be afraid of it. Include a picture of the animal.

Make a Mobile of Bats

Choose three or four different kinds of bats. Draw them on cardboard or heavy paper and cut them out. Thread them with different lengths of thread and hang them from a wire coat hanger.

Find Out More

There are many different kinds of bats. What kind of bats live in your part of the country? If no bats live where you live, find out about another kind of animal in your area that likes the nighttime, such as owls or raccoons.

123

STUDY SKILLS

READ TOGETHER

Use a Chart

Kind of Bat	Wingspan	Where It Lives
big brown bat	12 inches	North America
little brown bat	8 inches	North America
flying fox	5 feet	Australia
common vampire bat	12 inches	Central America and South America

Use the chart to answer the questions.

1 Where does the common vampire bat live?

2 What is the difference in size between the little brown bat and the big brown bat?

3 Which bat has the largest wingspan? How wide is it?

4 Which bats live in North America?

5 How do you think the flying fox got its name?

124

TEST POWER

Tell the story to yourself again, but use your own words.

DIRECTIONS:

Read the story. Then read each question about the story.

SAMPLE

A Trip to the Beach

Leslie and Michelle jumped out of the car. They couldn't wait to see the sand and the water. This was a very special trip for both of them. They had never been to the ocean before.

When they reached the beach, Michelle said, "This is great!" The sand was warm. Leslie's father sat on a towel and read a book. Michelle and Leslie began to build a sand castle right next to the water. The cool water splashed their toes. Leslie's mother watched them from under her beach umbrella.

In a few hours, they all were tired. They walked back up the hill to their car. "Let's come back again soon!" Leslie said.

1 The sand at the beach was—
   ○ colder than ice
   ○ full of rocks
   ○ wetter than before
   ○ warmer than the water was

2 Which conclusion can you draw from this story?
   ○ The beach is a good place on a hot day.
   ○ The beach is too rough for swimming.
   ○ The beach is full of people.
   ○ There are many rocks in the water at the beach.

Neighbors

If I lie down flat where the tall grass grows
    I can watch all the passersby—
The ants, the spiders, and other small things
    That creep and that run and that fly.

As long as I stay very quiet and still
    They do not mind if I stare.
They like to have me down in the grass
    Watching their travels there.

by Marchette Chute

What Is It?

It has no teeth,
so it can't eat a carrot.
It can't speak a word,
so it isn't a parrot.

It woggles and goggles
and scrunches its eyes.
It squawks and it yawps,
it burps and it cries.

It waggles its fingers,
it snuffles its nose.
Let's wait for a while
And watch how it grows.

by Eve Merriam

Try a Little Music

If you feel sad or scared today,
    Try a little music.
If things don't seem to go your way,
    Try a little music.
You'll feel better when you hear
That music pouring in your ear.
    So tum your drum
    And toot your flute,
And try a little music.

The Brothers Grimm

Jacob and Wilhelm Grimm were born in Germany more than 200 years ago. They heard old fairy tales from friends and shopkeepers. They wrote down all the stories so they would not be forgotten. Some of the fairy tales the Brothers Grimm collected are *Rapunzel*, *Hansel and Gretel*, and *Little Red Riding Hood*. Jacob and Wilhelm worked closely together. Jacob said, "Up to the very end, we worked in two rooms next to each other, always under one roof."

Meet Margaret H. Lippert

Margaret Lippert is a professional storyteller. She has retold many classic tales and has also written new stories.

Meet Mary GrandPré

Mary GrandPré has illustrated several books for children, including *Pockets*, the award-winning *Chin Yu Min and the Ginger Cat*, *Batwings and the Curtain of Night*, and *The Thread of Life: Twelve Old Italian Tales*.

The Bremen Town Musicians

The Brothers Grimm folktale

Retold by Margaret H. Lippert

Illustrated by Mary GrandPré

The Players

Donkey	Boss
Dog	Muscles
Cat	Curly
Rooster	Storyteller

ACT ONE

Storyteller: There was once a farmer who had a donkey. The donkey had worked hard for many years, but now he was getting too old to work. One day the farmer was talking to a friend about selling his donkey, and the donkey heard him.

Donkey: I can't believe that after all my hard work, the farmer has decided to sell me. No one will want to buy an old donkey like me. I think I will run away to Bremen Town and be a musician there.

Storyteller: So in the morning the donkey set off down the road to Bremen. Soon he came to a dog lying in the road.

Donkey: Why are you lying in the road?

Dog: I need to rest. I have just run a long, long way and I am very tired.

Donkey: Where are you going?

Dog: I don't know. I am running away because my master is angry with me. I am getting old and can't run as fast as I once could. Last night when I let a fox run off with a nice, plump chicken, my master told his daughter to kiss me good-bye. He said that I am no longer worth the food I eat, so I decided to run away.

Donkey: Why don't you come with me? I am going to Bremen to be a musician in the town band. You, too, have a beautiful voice. We can be in the town band together. I'll bray and you'll bark, and they will invite us to join.

Storyteller: So the dog and the donkey went along together. Soon they came to a cat who was looking very sad.

Donkey: Why are you so sad?

Cat: I am about to die. Last night I heard the miller talking to his family. He said he doesn't want me anymore because I am getting too old to catch mice. My teeth are not as sharp as they once were, so the mice get away. The miller said he is going to toss me into the lake tomorrow, and I can't swim.

Donkey: Don't be sad any longer. Come along with us. We are off to Bremen Town to be musicians in the town band. With your beautiful meow, you can be in the band, too.

Storyteller: So the cat followed the donkey and the dog down the road. Before long they saw a rooster crowing.

Donkey: I never heard a rooster crowing so late in the morning. What is the matter?

Rooster: Soon I will leave the earth, and this is my last song. I just heard the farmer tell his wife that I am getting old and sleep too late to wake them up in the morning. He told her to make me into soup for the family dinner.

Donkey: Why, then, you must come with us! We are going to Bremen to be musicians in the town band. With your crowing to add to my braying, the dog's barking, and the cat's meowing, we will be the envy of all the other musicians there.

Storyteller: So the rooster decided to join the donkey, the dog, and the cat, and they all went down the road together.

ACT TWO

Storyteller: The friends traveled on and on, but they did not reach Bremen that day. When it began to get dark, they decided to look for a place to spend the night. Way back in the woods they saw a little light. They went toward it, into the dark woods, hoping to find shelter. After a long time they saw a house through the trees.

Donkey: There must be someone at home. You hide behind this clump of bushes, while I go and look through the window.

Storyteller: The donkey went to the house and peeked in the window. There he saw a band of robbers eating dinner. On the table were stacks of gold coins and plates piled high with food. The donkey got an idea.

Donkey: This is the place for us. Now all we have to do is scare the robbers away.

Storyteller: The donkey went back to the other animals behind the bushes, and together they made a plan. First the donkey went and stood under the window. Then the dog climbed on the donkey's back, the cat climbed on the dog's back, and finally the rooster flew up on top of the cat's back. All at once they began to sing together loudly. As they were singing with all their might, the four animals lost their balance and toppled through the window. The robbers were so scared by all that noise that they ran out of the house and into the woods.

Donkey: We did it! We scared the robbers with our singing!

Dog: Look at all this good food. Come on, I'm ready to eat. Let's dig in.

Storyteller: Then the cat, the dog, the donkey, and the rooster all sat down at the table and ate until they were full.

Cat: My, but I'm tired. The fireplace is still warm. I think I'll curl up and go to sleep there.

Dog: I think I'll sleep here in this cozy spot behind the door.

Donkey: I'll go outside and sleep in front of the house.

Rooster: I think I'll take my nap up on the roof. Good night, all!

Storyteller: It was not long before all the animals were asleep. As the robbers began to think about the tasty dinner and the shiny gold they left behind, they decided they had made a mistake and had been scared away too quickly. They went back to the house and discovered that it was dark and quiet.

Boss: It looks as though our house is empty now. Let's go back in.

Muscles: No so fast, Boss. One of us should go in first to be sure all of them are gone. How about it, Curly?

Curly: Don't look at me, Muscles. I always have to do all the hard work.

Boss: He's right. You go ahead, Muscles. Look all around. If everything seems fine, whistle. When we hear you whistle, we'll come in. Good luck, and be careful.

Curly: Don't forget to open the front door slowly so it doesn't squeak.

Storyteller: Boss and Curly waited behind a clump of trees while Muscles went into the house. They were listening for a whistle, but Muscles never whistled. He was careful, but when he opened the front door it did squeak a little.

The cat opened her eyes. Muscles saw the cat's eyes gleaming like fire. He came closer to the fireplace to get more light, but instead he got the fright of his life. The cat jumped up and scratched him with her claws. As Muscles backed out of the door, the dog grabbed him by the leg. Then the donkey chased him out into the yard.

Muscles: Help! Help! I'm going to die.

Rooster (from the roof): COCK-A-DOODLE-DOO!

Storyteller: Muscles ran away and banged right into the other robbers, who were still standing behind the trees.

Boss: What happened? You look awful.

Muscles: I FEEL awful. My leg is bleeding and I'm hurting all over. I envy you, Curly. You have all the luck.

Curly: Well, don't be shy. Tell us what happened.

Muscles: There's a band of strong and angry people in there. One in the fireplace scratched me, another one behind the door grabbed my leg, and a third one chased me. Another one on the roof called out, "CATCH THAT MAN NOW, DO!"

Boss: Let's get out of here before they really do us some harm. We'll never come back again.

Storyteller: The robbers ran into the woods and never did go back. But the cat, the dog, the donkey, and the rooster had found exactly what they wanted—a warm, dry house to sleep in, and enough food stored up to last them a long time. They may live there still, making beautiful music together under the stars.

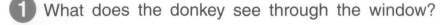

1 What does the donkey see through the window?

2 Why have the animals run away from home?

3 How are four old farm animals able to stand up to a band of robbers?

4 What is this story mostly about?

5 The characters in "The Bremen Town Musicians" and "Lemonade for Sale" both have something they want to do. What do they want to do? How do they do it?

Write a Report

Write a report about going to a concert or a play. It could be something you saw at school or a place you went with your family. At the beginning of your report, explain what the concert or play was mainly about.

146

Picture a Band

In "The Bremen Town Musicians," the four animals use their voices as musical instruments. Suppose you were going to start a band. Draw a picture of the instruments in your band. Label each instrument.

Make a Mask

Choose one character from "The Bremen Town Musicians." Make a mask for that character. You can use the directions on page 148 to help you.

Find Out More

The animals in the play use their voices as instruments. There is a kind of music where people use just their voices to make songs. This is called *a cappella* singing. It means singing without instruments. What kind of music do you like best? Find out how and where it started. Did it come from another country? Is it a new type of music? Has it been around for a hundred years?

147

STUDY SKILLS

READ TOGETHER

Follow Directions

The directions tell how to make a cat mask.

1. Find a large grocery bag. Cut eye holes about 3 inches from the top.

2. Cut a nose shape out of paper. Cut two ear shapes out of paper.

3. Glue the nose and ears into place.

4. Draw or paint whiskers, a mouth, and a tongue on the bag.

1 What materials do you need to make the cat mask?

2 What is the last step in the directions?

3 Could you do step 3 before you do step 2? Explain.

4 Suppose you wanted to make a dog mask. How might it be different from the cat mask?

5 Suppose you wanted to make a rooster mask. How could you make the rooster's beak?

Pay attention to the details in the story.

DIRECTIONS:

Read the story. Then read each question about the story.

SAMPLE

Building a Tree House

Mark was happy. It was Saturday. On Saturdays, Kim came over to work on the tree house.

Mark's father picked out a big tree in the backyard. Then, they bought wood and nails. Mark's father showed them how to use a hammer.

Every week Mark and Kim worked on the tree house. First, they built the floor. Then, they built the walls and roof. Now, the tree house was almost finished.

Kim brought a rug. They put it on the tree house floor.

Kim and Mark sat down on the rug. They looked around at their new tree house. They felt very proud. They had built it all by themselves!

1 Where did Kim and Mark build their tree house?

○ In Mark's bedroom
○ In Kim's backyard
○ In Mark's backyard
○ In the woods

2 What is the best summary for this story?

○ Mark and Kim put a rug in their tree house.
○ Mark and Kim are brother and sister.
○ Mark and Kim built a tree house in Mark's backyard.
○ Mark and Kim worked very hard on Saturdays.

Game Time

Toot! Toot! The whistle blows,
  It's time to start the game.
Red team runs on the field,
  Blue team does the same.
Zoom! Zoom! The ball goes fast,
  Blue team makes a score.
Boom! Boom! the band plays loudly,
  And all the people roar.

OUR SOCCER LEAGUE

BY CHUCK SOLOMON

WE'RE THE FALCONS.
WE PLAY SOCCER!

153

Today the game is with our friends, the Sluggers. They wear blue shirts.

First everyone stretches.

Then we practice.

In soccer, you dribble the ball with your feet.

You pass to your teammates.

And you try to kick the ball through the goal, if you can.

Goalies need practice, too. They stop the other team from scoring, and they're the only players on the field who can touch the ball with their hands.

It's game time!

The coaches give us our positions for the opening kickoff.

The Sluggers kick off and burst downfield. They charge to the goal. There's a goal kick.

Defense! Our goalie, Toby, makes a save. Toby throws it out, and we have the ball.

Eric dribbles to midfield . . . with the Sluggers in pursuit. Eric passes . . .

but a Slugger intercepts! He gets his foot behind the ball . . . and boots it!

The Sluggers have the ball.

But then it is kicked out-of-bounds. Whenever a team puts the ball out, the other team throws it back in.

Moira throws it in for us.

"Don't use your hands, Johnny!"

Eric booms it.

Score! It's one to nothing, Falcons.

Teams	1st half	2nd half	Final
Falcons	1		
Sluggers			

But not for long.

The Sluggers bounce right back and tie the game.

It's now one to one.

Teams	1st half	2nd half	Final
Falcons	1		
Sluggers	1		

The score is still tied at one to one when the coaches call halftime.

Whew! It feels good to take a break.

After a ten-minute rest . . .

we're back to the game!

We charge down to the Slugger's goal.

Olivier's kick is wide . . .

and the Sluggers take the ball.

161

Here comes our defense
at midfield.
    The two players collide.

    It's anybody's ball.

    The Sluggers and Falcons
battle for the ball.

    The ball goes up . . .

Joely kicks it . . .

Oh, no! "Hand ball!" Since a Slugger touched the ball, we get a free kick.

Jonathan booms it and we have control again.

No one scored, and the clock is running out. Only five minutes are left in the game.

5:00

4:00

2:00

Out-of-bounds on a header.

Ted throws it in.

The Sluggers boot the ball
into the open field.

1:00

John's set . . . boom!

Score! It's two to one,
Sluggers!

We try our best to tie the score . . .

but the clock runs out.

Teams	1st half	2nd half	Final
Falcons	1	0	1
Sluggers	1	1	2

The Sluggers celebrate . . .

and we give ourselves
a cheer.
When you play a great
game . . .

everybody wins!

MEET CHUCK SOLOMON

"I wanted to write *Our Soccer League* because soccer is such a good sport for children," says Chuck Solomon. "Soccer doesn't require much equipment, it's not too rough, and running is good exercise. Besides, both girls and boys can play it together."

Mr. Solomon wrote this book to show children how to play soccer. He said, "I also wanted to show the excitement and feelings you get when you play the game.

"I photographed this book during an actual game, just as it happens in the book. As I was taking pictures, an editor was writing what was happening. After I developed the photographs, I wrote the story. It was important for me to tell the story just the way it happened."

Story Questions & Activities

1 Which team wins the soccer game?

2 Why do you think the Falcons give themselves a cheer at the end of the game?

3 How are the photographs important to the story?

4 What is the main idea of this selection?

5 Imagine that Jamaica is teaching Luka to play soccer. What are some of the things she would tell her about how to play the game?

Write a Game Guide

Choose a favorite sport, game, or activity. Write a guide that explains how to play, do, or make what you chose. What are the rules of the game or the steps for the activity? What does each player do?

Make a Tally Chart About Favorite Sports

Which sport is the favorite of your class? Write down a guess. Then have a class vote to check your guess. Make a tally chart that shows how many votes each sport gets.

Describe a Sport

Find photographs of people playing a sport you like. What do the pictures tell you? Describe the action in the photographs. How is the sport you chose different from soccer? How is it like soccer?

Find Out More

Use an encyclopedia or sports book to find the name of each player's position, such as goal keeper and left defender. Draw a diagram of two soccer teams lining up for an opening kickoff. Label each position on the field. Use the diagram in "Our Soccer League" as a guide.

Read a Newsletter

SOCCER TODAY!

The Soccer Newsletter of Fairview County   October 15

Fairview County Soccer Club Goes to Moscow!

by Michael Tyler

In August, kids from the Fairview County Soccer Club went to Russia! The Fairview players were part of a special event. They played in the first game of a new soccer league for kids.

In some ways, the game they played was like opening games at home. There were parades, banners, and proud parents. But there was one big difference. It is a lot colder in Moscow than it is in Fairview County. That's because Moscow is farther north than Fairview County.

The weather was the only thing that was cold. The people in Moscow were warm and friendly. They look forward to meeting other kids from the U.S.

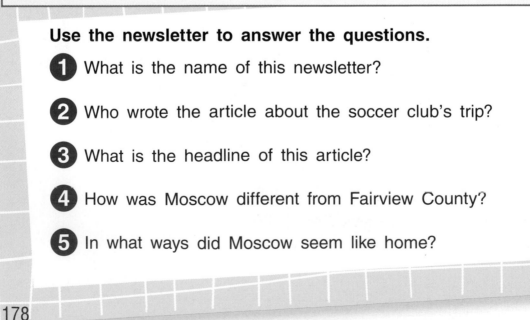

Use the newsletter to answer the questions.

1 What is the name of this newsletter?

2 Who wrote the article about the soccer club's trip?

3 What is the headline of this article?

4 How was Moscow different from Fairview County?

5 In what ways did Moscow seem like home?

TEST POWER

Ask yourself the questions again, but use your own words.

DIRECTIONS:

Read the story. Then read each question about the story.

SAMPLE

A Surprise Visitor

Elsa finished her homework. Her father was washing the dishes. Her mother had gone to dinner with a friend. She had left more than an hour ago and would be home soon.

"Can I help with the dishes?" Elsa asked her father. Just then, the front doorbell rang. Elsa's father walked to the front door. "Who is it?" he asked politely.

"It's a surprise," said a voice from outside. Elsa's father looked through the peephole. There was Elsa's mother and Elsa's grandma.

"Surprise!" yelled her grandma as Elsa ran to give her a hug.

1 Which is the best summary for this story?
○ Elsa has a surprise birthday party.
○ Elsa and her dad have dinner together.
○ Elsa has a surprise visitor.
○ Elsa's grandma moves away.

2 What happens after Elsa's father opens the door?
○ Elsa sees her neighbor.
○ Elsa sees her grandma.
○ Elsa runs to hide.
○ Elsa's father sees his brother.

To Market! To Market!

To market, to market
With Grandmother today.
We go hand in hand
And we giggle all the way.
The basket we carry
Gets filled to the top,
With things that we buy
From each place that we stop.
And when we go home
Grandmother puts up her feet,
Time to listen to a story
And have something to eat.

THE WEDNESDAY SURPRISE

by Eve Bunting

I like surprises. But the one Grandma and I are planning for Dad's birthday is the best surprise of all.

illustrated by Donald Carrick

We work on it Wednesday nights. On Wednesdays Mom has to stay late at the office and my brother, Sam, goes to basketball practice at the Y. That's when Grandma rides the bus across town to stay with me.

I watch for her from the window and I blow on the glass to make breath pictures while I wait. When I see her I call: "Sam! She's here!" and he says it's okay to run down, down the long stairs and wait by the door.

"Grandma!" I call.

"Anna!" She's hurrying, her big, cloth bag bumping against her legs.

We meet and hug. She tells me how much I've grown since last week and I tell her how much she's grown, too, which is our joke. Between us we carry her lumpy bag upstairs.

I show Grandma my breath picture, if it's still there. Mostly she knows what it is. Mostly she's the only one who does.

On Wednesday nights we have hot dogs.

"Have you heard from your dad?" Grandma asks Sam.

"He'll be back Saturday, same as always," Sam says. "In time for his birthday."

"His birthday?" Grandma raises her eyebrows as if she'd forgotten all about that.

Grandma is some actress!

When Sam goes she and I do the dishes. Then we get down to business.

I sit beside her on the couch and she takes the first picture book from the bag. We read the story together, out loud, and when we finish one book we start a second.

We read for an hour, get some ice cream, then read some more.

Grandma gives me another hug. "Only seven years old and smart as paint already!"

I'm pleased. "They're all going to be so surprised on Saturday," I say.

When Sam comes home we play card games, and when Mom comes she plays, too.

"You'll be here for the birthday dinner?" Mom asks as Grandma is getting ready to leave.

"Oh yes, the birthday," Grandma says vaguely, as if she'd forgotten again. As if we hadn't been working on our special surprise for weeks and weeks. Grandma is tricky.

"I'll be here," she says.

Sam walks Grandma to the bus stop. As they're going down the stairs I hear him say: "What have you got in this bag, Grandma? Bricks?"

That makes me smile.

Dad comes home Saturday morning, and we rush at him with our *Happy Birthdays*. He has brought Sam a basketball magazine and me a pebble, smooth and speckled as an egg, for my rock collection.

"I found it in the desert, close to the truck stop," he says. "It was half covered with sand."

I hold it, imagining I can still feel the desert sun hot inside it. How long did it lie there? What kind of rock is it?

ad has stopped to pick wildflowers for Mom. They're wilting and she runs to put them in water. Then Dad has to go to bed because he has been driving his big truck all through the night.

While Dad sleeps, Sam and I hang red and blue streamers in the living room. We help Mom frost the cake. We've made Dad's favorite dinner, pot roast, and our gifts are wrapped and ready.

I watch for Grandma and help carry the bag upstairs. Wow! Sam should feel how heavy it is now! Grandma has brought a ton of books. We hide the bag behind the couch. I am sick from being nervous.

randma usually has seconds but tonight she doesn't. I don't either. I can tell Mom is worried about the pot roast but Grandma tells her it's very good.

"Are you feeling well, Mama?" Dad asks Grandma. "How are your knees?"

"Fine. Fine. The knees are fine."

Dad blows out the birthday candles and we give him his gifts. Then Grandma shoots a glance in my direction and I go for the big bag and drag it across to the table. I settle it on the floor between us.

"Another present?" Dad asks.

"It's a special surprise for your birthday, Dad, from Grandma and me."

My heart's beating awfully fast as I unzip the bag and give the first book to Grandma. It's called *Popcorn*. I squeeze Grandma's hand and she stands and begins to read.

Mom and Dad and Sam are all astonished.

Dad jumps up and says: "What's this?" but Mom shushes him and pulls him back down.

Grandma has the floor. She finishes *Popcorn*, which takes quite a while, gives the book back to me and beams all over her face.

"My goodness!" Mom is beaming too. "When did this wonderful thing happen? When did you learn to read?"

"Anna taught me," Grandma says.

"On Wednesday nights," I add. "And she took the books home, and practiced."

"You were always telling me to go to classes, classes, classes," Grandma says to Dad. She looks at Mom. "You must learn to read, you say. So? I come to Anna."

I giggle because I'm so excited.

Grandma reads and acts out *The Easter Pig*. And *The Velveteen Rabbit*.

"It's much smarter if you learn to read when you're young," she tells Sam sternly. "The chance may pass along with the years."

Sam looks hurt. "But I *can* read, Grandma."

"Nevertheless." She takes out another book.

"Are you going to read everything in that bag, Mama?" Dad asks her. He's grinning, but his eyes are brimming over with tears and he and Mom are holding hands across the table.

"Maybe I will read everything in the world now that I've started," Grandma says in a stuck-up way. "I've got time." She winks at me.

"So, Anna? What do you think? Was it a good surprise?"

I run to her and she puts her cheek against mine. "The best ever," I say.

Meet
Eve Bunting

There's a story about *The Wednesday Surprise,* and Eve Bunting tells about it like this: "A friend took me out to dinner and began talking about her mother, Katina, who was quite a character.

"She told a story about how she taught her mother to read English with her picture books. Every day she would bring books home from school or the library, and they would read them together. *The Wednesday Surprise* is my book, but it's Katina's story."

Ms. Bunting loves Donald Carrick's illustrations. She asked him if the kitchen in *The Wednesday Surprise* was like his kitchen. He said to her, "Oh, yes. There's always a bit of my house in my books."

THE WALL
by Eve Bunting
illustrated by Ronald Himler

Fly Away Home
By Eve Bunting; illustrated by Ronald Himler

Meet DONALD CARRICK

Donald Carrick started drawing pictures as a child, and he kept on drawing his whole life. His first job was painting signs and billboards. Later, he painted pictures for newspaper and magazine ads. His wife, Carol, wrote the first children's book he ever illustrated, *The Old Barn.* After that, Donald Carrick illustrated more than eighty picture books. Some of the most popular ones are about a boy named Christopher and his two dogs. Two other well-known books are about a boy named Patrick who imagines there are dinosaurs everywhere.

207

What is the surprise that Anna and Grandma have planned for Dad's birthday?

 Why does Anna's dad cry at the surprise party?

 How does Anna feel after Grandma starts to read?

 What is this story mainly about?

5 Compare the gift Fernando gives Carmina in "Fernando's Gift" to Grandma's gift to Dad. What makes these gifts special?

Write About a Book

Write a report about a book you like. Include the names of the author and illustrator. Explain what the book is about and what happens in it. Include a beginning, middle, and end in your book report.

16

Make a Calendar

Anna needed to know how many days she and Grandma had to work on their surprise. A calendar would tell her. Make a calendar for yourself. Mark important days such as holidays, birthdays, and vacation dates.

Make a Book Cover

Books are very important to Grandma and Anna. Make a book cover to protect your favorite book. Use brown paper bags or large sheets of paper to wrap your book. Draw a scene from the book for the front cover. On the back write: This book belongs to [your name goes here].

Find Out More

Birthdays can be special days. What are some other special days that you and your family celebrate? Choose a holiday and find out more about it. Write a postcard to a friend telling what makes the day special.

To:
My Special Friend

Use a Calendar

Anna and Grandma use this calendar to plan their surprise. Anna marks off with an X each day that passes.

March

Sunday	Monday	Tuesday	Wednesday	Thursday	Friday	Saturday
				1 ✕	2 ✕	3 ✕
4 ✕	5 ✕	6 ✕	7 Practice reading	8 ✕	9 ✕	10 ✕
11 ✕	12 ✕	13 ✕	14 Practice reading	15 ✕	16 ✕	17 ✕
18	19 Get new books	20	21 Practice reading	22	23	24
25	26	27	28 Practice reading	29	30 Bake cake	31 Dad's party

1. When will Anna and Grandma get new books?

2. How many days do Grandma and Anna practice reading in all?

3. How many reading days do they have left?

4. How many days are left until Dad's party?

5. On what day should Grandma and Anna mail party invitations? How many days before the party is that?

TEST POWER

Read each answer before you choose the best one.

DIRECTIONS:

Read the story. Then read each question about the story.

SAMPLE

A Trip for Science Class

Our class took a trip to the beach to study the seashore. Each person had a partner. Our teacher, Mr. Ranja, gave us a list of things to look for. Mr. Ranja told us to write down what we learned.

---

1. Find three different shells. What makes each one different?

2. Look carefully at the sand. What does it look like? Is it soft or hard?

3. Look at the seaweed. What does it look like? What other plants do you see on the beach?

---

1 What are the students supposed to do first?

○ Look at plants
○ Find three different shells
○ Look at the sand
○ Find ten different shells

2 What's the best summary for this story?

○ Mr. Ranja's class looked at many things at the beach.
○ The sand at the beach is hard.
○ Mr. Ranja's class took a trip to the museum.
○ We had partners at the beach.

Digging

Digging deep, digging down,
I dug a big hole in the ground.
Soil black, soil brown,
Look at all the things I found.
 A little seashell white as snow,
 A toy I lost two years ago.
 A piece of someone's broken dish,
 A fossil shaped just like a fish.
Digging, digging in the ground,
Oh, what special things I found!

MEET Aliki

Looking back at why she became an artist, Aliki says that one day in kindergarten, her life changed forever. That day, Aliki showed two pictures she had made, one of her family and one of Peter Rabbit's family. "Such a fuss was made over them," she says, that she was never the same again.

Aliki says "I'm one of those lucky people who love what they do." Part of what she enjoys about creating children's books is blending pictures and words to make hard ideas easier to understand.

When writing nonfiction works like *Fossils Tell of Long Ago*, she says, "It's best for me to know nothing about a subject when I begin... that way I have to get it right."

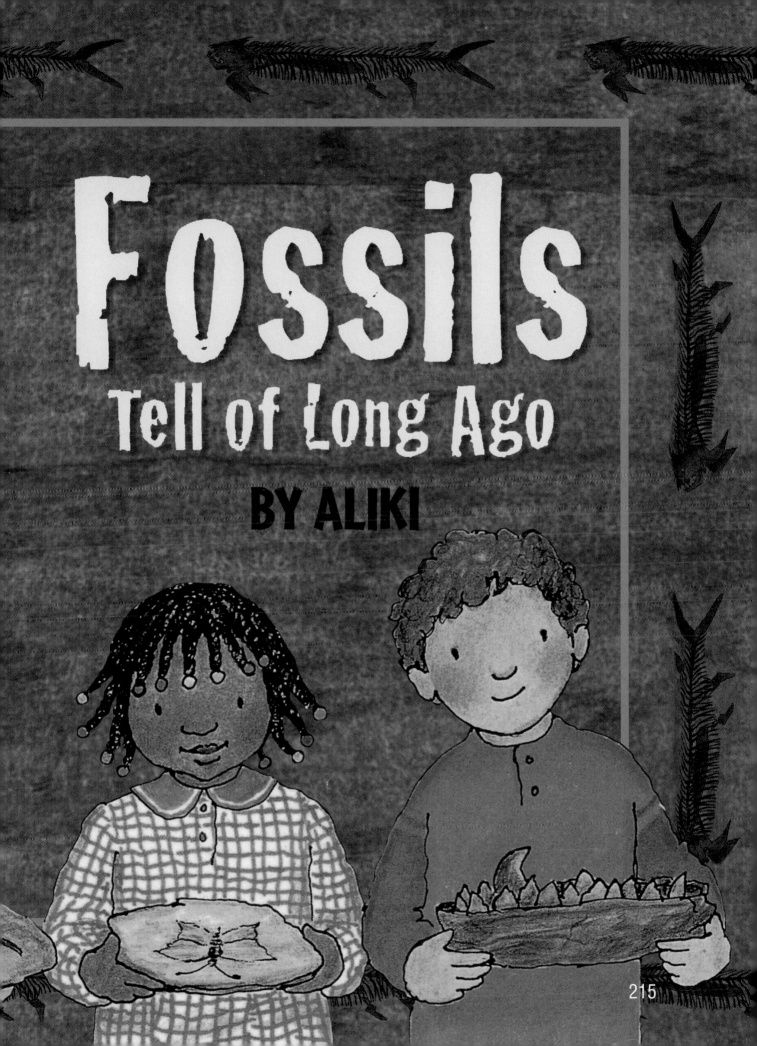

Fossils
Tell of Long Ago

BY ALIKI

Once upon a time a huge fish was swimming
around when along came a smaller fish.

The big fish was so hungry it swallowed the
other fish whole.

The big fish died and sank to the bottom
of the sea. This happened ninety million years
ago. How do we know?

Fossils tell us about the past. Fossils tell us there once were forests where now there are deserts.

Fossils tell us there once were seas where now there are mountains. Many lands that are cold today were once warm. We find fossils of tropical plants in very cold places.

225

Fossils tell us about strange creatures that lived on earth long ago. No such creatures are alive today. They have all died out. We say they are extinct.

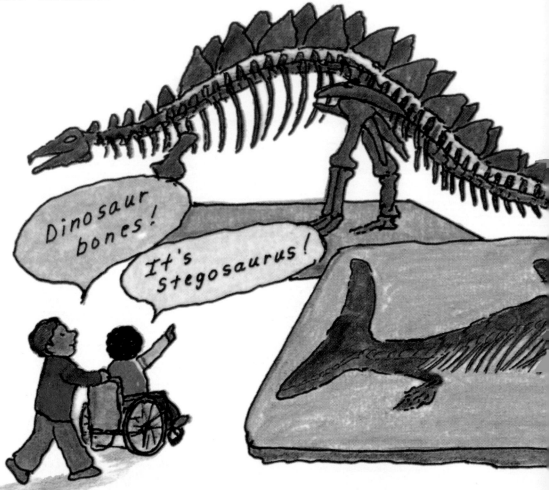

Dinosaur bones!

It's Stegosaurus!

Some fossils are found by scientists who dig for them. Some fossils are found by accident. You, too, might find a fossil if you look hard. When you see a stone, look at it carefully. It may be a fossil of something that once lived.

227

How would you like to make a fossil? Not a one-million-year-old fossil. A one-minute-old fossil. Make a clay imprint of your hand.

The imprint shows what your hand is like, the way a dinosaur's track shows us what its foot was like.

First you take some clay.

Then you flatten it out.

Press your hand in the clay.

Then lift your hand away.

Suppose, when it dried out, you buried your clay imprint. Suppose, a million years from now, someone found it. Your imprint would be as hard as stone. It would be a fossil of your hand. It would tell the finder something about you. It would tell something about life on earth a million years earlier.

Every time someone finds a fossil, we learn more about life on earth long ago.

Someday you may find a fossil—one that is millions and millions of years old.

You may discover something
no one knows today.

Story Questions & Activities

1 What is a fossil?

2 Has Earth changed much since the dinosaurs?

3 Why are fossils important to scientists?

4 What is the main idea of this selection?

5 Where do you think Amanda from "The Best Vacation Ever" might have found fossils?

Write a Speech

What if you found a fossil? Write a speech that tells all about your discovery. What is your fossil made of? How did it become a fossil? What else can you learn from your fossil?

Make a Fossil

Make a clay imprint of your hand. Flatten some clay. Press your hand in the clay. Take your hand away. Carve your name and today's date underneath your handprint. Let the clay dry out and harden for a few days before moving your fossil.

Create a Mural

Fossils can tell us about the plants and animals that lived in a particular place. What plants and animals live in your community? Plan a mural that shows some of these plants and animals. Remember to add a title and to sign the mural in the corner.

Find Out More

Giant dinosaurs roamed Earth long before humans did. Find out more about dinosaurs. Choose a dinosaur to research and write a list of facts about it. When did it live? What did it eat? About how big was it?

Interpret Signs

Fossils can tell us about animals and plants from the past. Many science museums have shows about fossils. This picture shows the main lobby of a science museum.

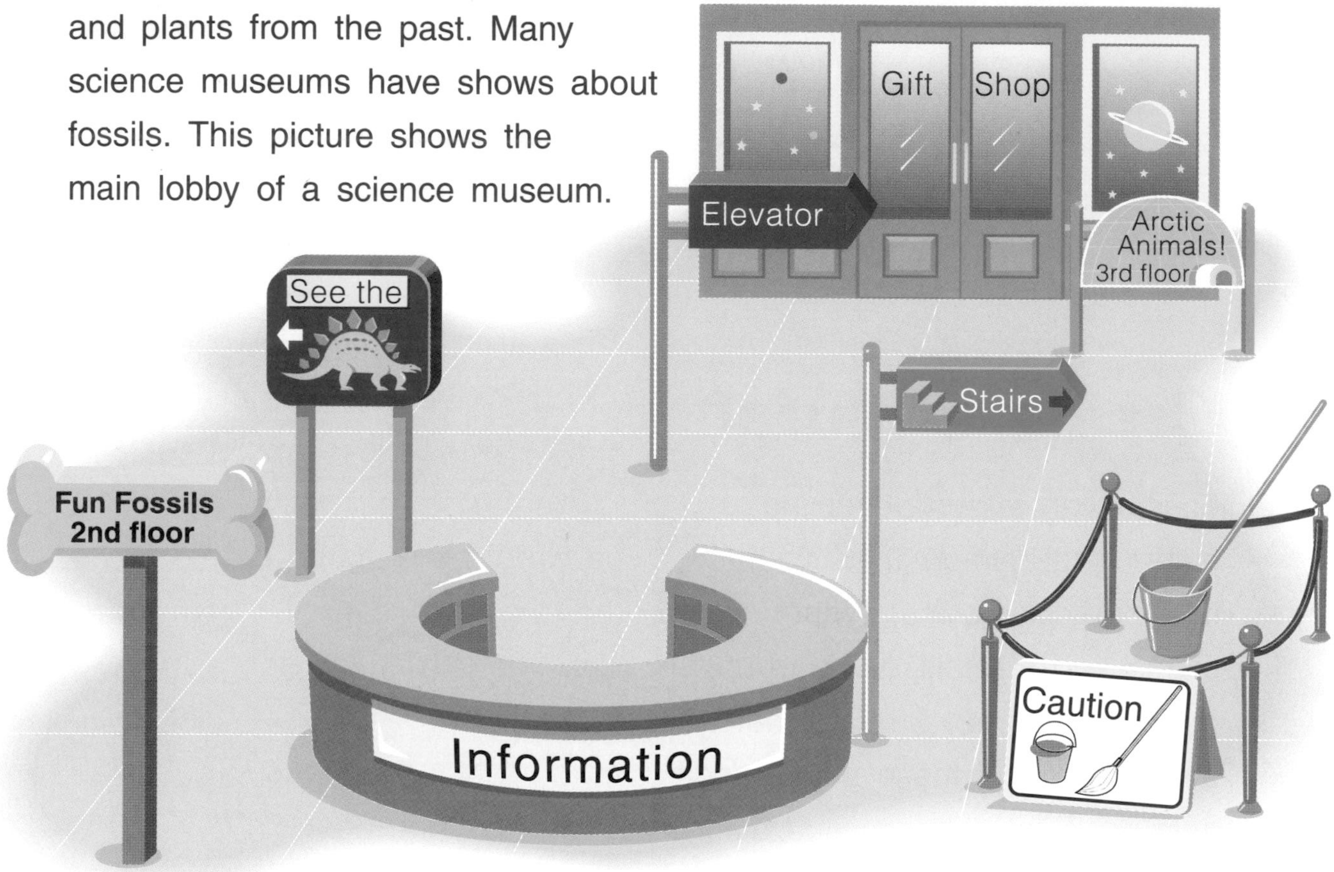

Gift Shop

Elevator

Arctic Animals! 3rd floor

See the

Stairs

Fun Fossils 2nd floor

Information

Caution

1 On which floor is the fossil exhibit?

2 Where is the gift shop?

3 Where would you ask for directions?

4 What does the sign near the ropes mean?

5 Do you think the dinosaur show is on the same floor as the lobby? Explain your answer.

TEST POWER

DIRECTIONS:

Read the story. Then read each question about the story.

SAMPLE

A Present for Dad

Marci and her mother went shopping to buy a present. They walked into the store. They asked a salesperson for help. The salesperson showed them a list of everything in the store.

	Floor
Men's Clothing	3
Men's Shoes	3
Boys' Clothing	2
Girls' Clothing	2
Women's Clothing	1
Women's Shoes	1

Marci and her mother went to the third floor. They found a red necktie that Marci liked. Marci took the tie home. She put it in a box. Then, she wrapped the box in blue paper.

She made a card for her dad and put it on top. The next day, Marci gave the present to her father. He liked it so much that he wore it that same day.

1 What is the best summary for this story?
○ Marci goes shopping for a present.
○ Marci and her mother like to shop.
○ Marci bought a box.
○ Marci likes the color red.

2 What did Marci and her mother do first?
○ They asked for help.
○ They took the tie home.
○ They bought shoes.
○ Marci made a card.

When You're an Archeologist

If you're digging up a clue
When you're an archeologist,
Then nothing new will do
When you're an archeologist.

Old toys could tell you how
Life happened up till now.
You can add them to your list
When you're an archeologist.

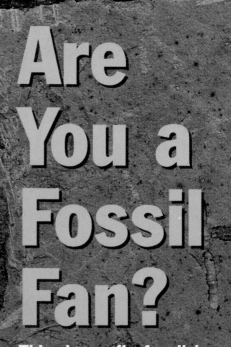

TIME FOR KIDS

Are You a Fossil Fan?

This dragonfly fossil is millions of years old.

The Fossil Kid

This boy has been digging since he was eight.

When Sam Girouard was eight years old, he visited his grandmother in Alabama. On that visit, Sam and his grandmother made a big discovery. They found all kinds of fossils. "Ferns, plants, things like that. I still have all those fossils," says Sam. Those fossils changed Sam's life forever.

Sam is now a teenager. He is also a scientist. Sam knows a lot about fossils. (Fossils are the remains of plants and animals that died a long time ago. Over time, the remains turned to stone.)

COVER: JOHN CANCALOSI/PETER ARNOLD; RIGHT: DAN LAMONT/MATRIX RIGHT: LAYNE KENNEDY/CORBIS; FAR RIGHT:

A T. rex dinosaur tooth is larger than a kid's hand.

Sam Girouard hunts for fossils near his home in Washington State.

239

Fossils of a fern, a bird, and a fish are each millions of years old.

Sam spends hours and hours digging for fossils. Once, Sam found a few tiny pieces of bone. Sam knew he had found something important. So he spent the day on his hands and knees looking for more bone. He picked up all the tiny pieces he could find. Then he glued them together. The pieces made up a dinosaur tooth. The dinosaur had lived millions of years ago!

Sam has found other kinds of fossils, too. He's found the wrist bone of an American mastodon. Tests showed that it was more than four million years old. It was the oldest American mastodon fossil ever found.

A large termite is trapped in amber. Amber comes from sticky tree sap. Bugs get trapped in it. Over time, it hardens into amber.

Sam has found a fossil of a raindrop. It is the only raindrop fossil ever found in Washington. He has also found a wing of a fly. The fly lived millions of years ago.

When Sam finds an unusual fossil, he writes about it for a magazine. The magazine is read by many scientists. Sometimes grown-up scientists are surprised to learn that Sam is a teenager. Sam says that if some scientists knew he was a kid, they would not take his work seriously. "I want people to see that I'm doing science. Then they can hear about my age," says Sam.

DID YOU KNOW?
FOSSIL FACTS

◆ The oldest reptile fossil nests ever found were discovered in Arizona. The nests are 220 million years old. The reptiles were cousins of today's crocodiles and turtles.

◆ Scientists study fossils to find out about the history of Earth and of the plants and animals that have lived here.

◆ You can find fossils in every state, and there are a lot to go around. But fossils tell only a small part of the story of all the plants and animals that have lived on Earth.

◆ The oldest fossils are about $3\frac{1}{2}$ billion years old.

FIND OUT MORE
Visit our website:
www.mhschool.com/reading

*inter*NET
CONNECTION

1 What animals and plant fossils did Sam find?

2 Why is the wrist bone of the American mastodon that Sam found so special?

3 Why do you think Sam wants people to read his work before they hear about his age?

4 What is the main idea of this selection?

5 Sam Girouard and the young riders of the Pony Express have done great things. What words might describe both Sam and the Pony Express riders?

Write a Report

Some people know very little about fossils. Write a magazine article that will help them learn about fossils. Explain what fossils are. Tell about some of the fossils Sam has found. Tell where and how he found the fossils.

Be a Fossil Finder

Imagine that you are a scientist who lives a million years from now. You have just made a fantastic fossil discovery that tells about life on Earth around the year 2000. What would you find? Write a short magazine article about your discovery.

Create Leaf Fossils

Collect several different leaves. Then make leaf rubbings to show what the fossils might look like. Follow these steps:

1. Lay the leaf with the underside face up on your desk.
2. Cover the leaf with tracing paper.
3. Rub the paper lightly with a soft pencil, a piece of charcoal, or a crayon.

Find Out More

Sam found the wrist bone of an American mastodon. Find out more about mastodons. What were they? When did they live? What did they look like? Draw a picture of a mastodon, and list three facts about it.

Read an Advertisement

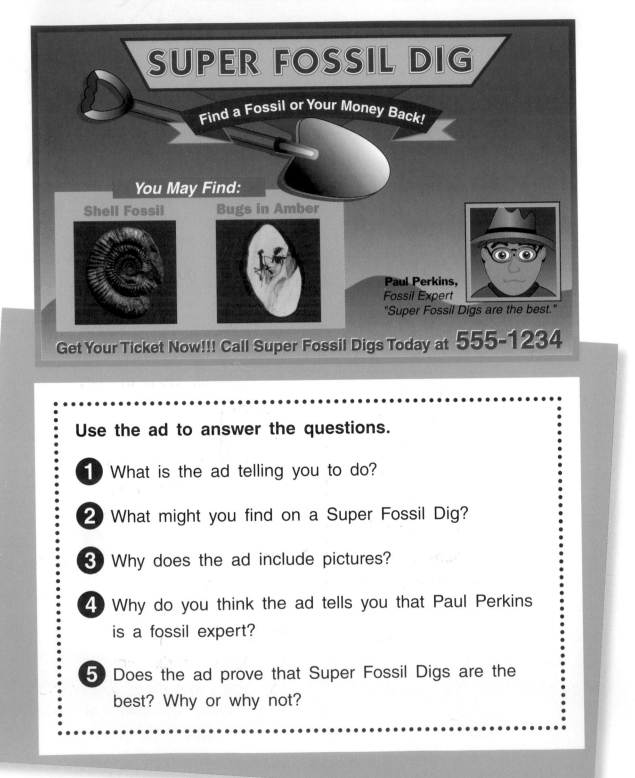

Use the ad to answer the questions.

1. What is the ad telling you to do?

2. What might you find on a Super Fossil Dig?

3. Why does the ad include pictures?

4. Why do you think the ad tells you that Paul Perkins is a fossil expert?

5. Does the ad prove that Super Fossil Digs are the best? Why or why not?

TEST POWER

Directions tell you what to do.

DIRECTIONS:
Read the story. Then read each question about the story.

SAMPLE

How to Make a Hand Puppet

Read all of the directions first. You will need:

   an old sock
   three buttons
   a red marker
   yarn, glue, and scissors

Put the sock on your hand. Open and close your hand. This will be the puppet's mouth. Draw a line around the mouth with the marker. Draw two dots on the top of the sock. Glue two buttons for the puppet's eyes here. Draw another dot where you want the nose to be. Glue the third button here. Cut twenty pieces of yarn. Each piece should be about six inches long. Glue the middle of each piece of yarn to the top of the sock for hair. Put the puppet aside for an hour so that the glue can dry.

1 What do the directions say to do after you draw the puppet's mouth?
   ○ Glue the buttons on.
   ○ Put the sock on your hand.
   ○ Find a sock to use.
   ○ Read the directions.

2 What do you do after you glue the yarn on?
   ○ Let the glue dry.
   ○ Draw the eyes.
   ○ Read the directions.
   ○ Open and close your hand.

To Catch a Fish

It takes more than a wish
to catch a fish
you take the hook
you add the bait
you concentrate
and then you wait
you wait you wait
but not a bite
the fish don't have
an appetite
so tell them what
good bait you've got
and how your bait
can hit the spot
this works a whole
lot better than
a wish
if you really
want to catch
a fish

by Eloise Greenfield

247

248

STARTING NOW

Which?

When I am in the country
I like the trees and grass.
I like the cows and horses,
I count them as I pass.

When I am in the city
I like the city streets.
I like the trucks and taxis
Passing by in fleets.

"The city or the country?"
I sometimes say to Mother,
"I cannot say which one I like
Better than the other."

by James S. Tippett

Scratch My Itch

Help! Help! Please help!
    I need an extra hand or two.
I have an itch that I can't reach,
    I don't know what to do.
And so, I have phoned you,
    To kindly help me catch
That middle-of-my-back itch
    That I cannot seem to scratch.
What's that? You say
    You also need help feeling fine?
Well, I'll be glad to scratch your back
    If you will then scratch mine.

MEET

PEGGY RATHMANN

Peggy Rathmann grew up outside St. Paul, Minnesota. Describing her childhood, she says, "When I was little, the highlight of the summer was running barefoot through the grass, in the dark, screaming."

When she grew up, Ms. Rathmann wanted to teach sign language to gorillas. After taking a class in sign language, "I realized what I'd rather do was draw pictures of gorillas," she says. And later, she did—in her book *Goodnight, Gorilla*.

Ms. Rathmann based her character Gloria on her parents' dog Skippy. Once, Skippy licked a whole platter of poached eggs before Rathmann's family ate them for breakfast!

OFFICER BUCKLE AND GLORIA

PEGGY RATHMANN

254

Officer Buckle knew more safety tips than anyone else in Napville.

Every time he thought of a new one, he thumbtacked it to his bulletin board.

Safety Tip #77

NEVER stand on a SWIVEL CHAIR.

Officer Buckle shared his safety
tips with the students at Napville
School.

Nobody ever listened.

Sometimes, there was snoring.

Afterward, it was business as usual.

Mrs. Toppel, the principal, took down the welcome banner.

"NEVER stand on a SWIVEL CHAIR," said Officer Buckle, but Mrs. Toppel didn't hear him.

Then one day, Napville's police
department bought a police dog named
Gloria.

When it was time for Officer Buckle
to give the safety speech at the school,
Gloria went along.

"Children, this is Gloria," announced
Officer Buckle. "Gloria obeys my commands.
Gloria, SIT!" And Gloria sat.

Officer Buckle gave Safety Tip
Number One:

"KEEP your SHOELACES tied!"

The children sat up and stared.

Officer Buckle checked to see
if Gloria was sitting at attention.
She was.

"Safety Tip Number Two," said Officer
Buckle. "ALWAYS wipe up spills BEFORE
someone SLIPS AND FALLS!"

The children's eyes popped.

Officer Buckle checked on Gloria again.

"Good dog," he said.

Officer Buckle thought of a safety
tip he had discovered that morning.

"NEVER leave a THUMBTACK where you might SIT on it!"

The audience roared.

Officer Buckle grinned. He said the rest of the tips with *plenty* of expression.

The children clapped their hands and cheered. Some of them laughed until they cried.

Officer Buckle was surprised. He had never noticed how funny safety tips could be.

After *this* safety speech, there wasn't a single accident.

The next day, an enormous envelope
arrived at the police station. It was stuffed
with thank-you letters from the students at
Napville School.

Every letter had a drawing of Gloria
on it.

Officer Buckle thought the drawings
showed a lot of imagination.

His favorite letter was written on
a star-shaped piece of paper. It said:

You and Gloria make a good team.

Your friend,
Claire

P.S. I always wear
a crash helmet.
(Safety Tip #7)

Officer Buckle was thumbtacking Claire's letter to his bulletin board when the phones started ringing. Grade schools, high schools, and day-care centers were calling about the safety speech.

"Officer Buckle," they said, "our students want to hear your safety tips! And please, bring along that police dog."

Officer Buckle told his safety tips to 313 schools.

Everywhere he and Gloria went, children sat up and listened.

After every speech, Officer Buckle
took Gloria out for ice cream.
Officer Buckle loved having a buddy.

Then one day, a television news team
videotaped Officer Buckle in the state-college
auditorium.

When he finished Safety Tip Number
Ninety-nine, DO NOT GO SWIMMING DURING
ELECTRICAL STORMS!, the students jumped to their
feet and applauded..

"Bravo! Bravo!" they cheered.
Officer Buckle bowed again and again.

That night, Officer Buckle watched
himself on the 10 o'clock news.

The next day, the principal of Napville School telephoned the police station.

"Good morning, Officer Buckle! It's time for our safety speech!"

Officer Buckle frowned.

"I'm not giving any more speeches! Nobody looks at me, anyway!"

"Oh," said Mrs. Toppel. "Well! How about Gloria? Could she come?"

Someone else from the police station gave
Gloria a ride to the school.

Gloria sat onstage looking lonely. Then
she fell asleep. So did the audience.

After Gloria left, Napville School had its
biggest accident ever . . . .

It started with a puddle of banana pudding . . . .

SPLAT!

SPLATTER!

SPLOOSH!

Everyone slid smack into Mrs. Toppel, who screamed and let go of her hammer.

The next morning, a pile of letters arrived at the police station. Every letter had a drawing of the accident.

Officer Buckle was shocked.

At the bottom of the pile was a note written on a paper star.

Officer Buckle smiled.

The note said:

Gloria gave Officer Buckle a big kiss on the nose. Officer Buckle gave Gloria a nice pat on the back. Then, Officer Buckle thought of his best safety tip yet . . .

Safety Tip #101

"ALWAYS STICK WITH YOUR BUDDY!"

1 What does Officer Buckle talk about when he visits schools?

2 Why do students start to pay attention to Officer Buckle's safety tips?

3 Do you think Officer Buckle's safety speeches are helpful? Explain.

4 What is this story mostly about?

5 If Gloria and Mudge could talk, what would they say about humans?

Write a Gloria Story

Gloria helps Officer Buckle see that making people laugh is a good way to get their attention. Write a funny story about a helpful friend. Tell the events in the order they happen.

Make Safety Tip Cards

Officer Buckle has lots of safety tips. Make up some of your own. Write three safety tips on index cards. Draw a picture to go with each one. Be original.

Draw Safety Signs

What safety signs have you seen in your neighborhood or near your school? Draw a picture of two safety signs. Then write one sentence about why these signs are important.

Find Out More

Gloria is a police dog who helps Officer Buckle. Find out more about working dogs. Name some other dogs that are specially trained to help humans? What do they do?

STUDY SKILLS *READ TOGETHER*

Do a Library Subject Search

> Enter the number of the search that you want:
>
> **1.** Names   **2.** Titles   **3.** Subjects

> Press number **3** for Subjects. Enter the subject that you want to search.

Type in BICYCLE SAFETY. Press ENTER.

Here are the results of your search.

Author and Title	Call Number and Format	Date
Bike on the Safe Side	J M16 2465 B [Movie]	1974
Gibbons, Gail *The Bicycle Book*	J 629.22 G	c 1995
Naden, Corrine J. *Bicycling Safely*	J 796.6 N	c 1979

Use the computer displays to answer the questions.

1 What subject are you researching?

2 The list has one movie. What is its title?

3 Who wrote *Bicycling Safely*?

4 Which book will have the newest information?

5 Which book will have the most information on bicycle safety? How do you know?

Tell the story again to yourself in your own words to make sure you understand it.

DIRECTIONS:

Read the story. Then read each question about the story.

SAMPLE

What Is a Penny For?

Katie went for a walk to the ice cream store. As she walked, she looked down at the sidewalk. She walked carefully over the bumps and cracks. Katie saw something shiny on the sidewalk. She picked it up. It was a brand new penny.

"A penny is good luck," said Katie. She put the penny in her pocket. Katie felt lucky already. "I wish that a penny was enough money for ice cream," thought Katie.

It started to rain. Katie turned around to go home. She walked into the house and went into the kitchen. There on the table was a bowl of ice cream just for her!

1 What does Katie find in this story?
   ○ A rabbit's foot
   ○ A penny
   ○ A friend's book
   ○ A raincoat

2 Which general statement can you make from this story?
   ○ Katie's house is like all other houses.
   ○ Sometimes you get what you wish for.
   ○ A penny buys a lot of ice cream.
   ○ It's hard to eat ice cream in the rain.

Magic Ticket

A library card might take you places
Near and far away.
Just check out a book and you
Can fly away today.
A book can take you to the stars
Or underneath the sea.
A library card is all you need,
And best of all, it's free.

MEET PAT MORA

Many of Pat Mora's ideas for stories come from her childhood days in the Texas desert. "I also like to write about my family, like my aunt who danced on her ninetieth birthday and my mother who wanted to be a rainbow tulip when she was in grade school," Ms. Mora says.

MEET RAUL COLÓN

Raul Colón likes to create many different kinds of art. He has illustrated several children's books, including *Always My Dad*, for which he won the Silver Medal from the Society of Illustrators.

A NOTE ABOUT THE STORY

Pat Mora based this story on Tomás Rivera, a real person. Rivera was a migrant farm worker. He was born in Crystal City, Texas, in 1935. Just like the boy in the story, Rivera felt education was very important. He grew up to be a writer, a teacher, and the leader of a university.

Tomás and the Library Lady

Illustrated by Raul Colón

by Pat Mora

It was midnight. The light of the full moon followed the tired old car. Tomás was tired too. Hot and tired. He missed his own bed, in his own house in Texas.

Tomás was on his way to Iowa again with his family. His mother and father were farm workers. They picked fruit and vegetables for Texas farmers in the winter and for Iowa farmers in the summer.

Year after year they bump-bumped along in their rusty old car. "Mamá," whispered Tomás, "if I had a glass of cold water, I would drink it in large gulps. I would suck the ice. I would pour the last drops of water on my face."

Tomás was glad when the car finally stopped. He helped his grandfather, Papá Grande, climb down. Tomás said, *"Buenas noches"*—"Good night"—to Papá, Mamá, Papá Grande, and to his little brother, Enrique. He curled up on the cot in the small house that his family shared with the other workers.

Early the next morning Mamá and Papá went out to pick corn in the green fields. All day they worked in the hot sun. Tomás and Enrique carried water to them. Then the boys played with a ball Mamá had sewn from an old teddy bear.

289

When they got hot, they sat under a tree with Papá Grande. "Tell us the story about the man in the forest," said Tomás.

Tomás liked to listen to Papá Grande tell stories in Spanish. Papá Grande was the best storyteller in the family.

"*En un tiempo pasado*," Papá Grande began. "Once upon a time . . . on a windy night a man was riding a horse through a forest. The wind was howling, *whooooooooo*, and the leaves were blowing, *whish, whish . . .*

"All of a sudden something grabbed the man. He couldn't move. He was too scared to look around. All night long he wanted to ride away. But he couldn't.

"How the wind howled, *whooooooooo*. How the leaves blew. How his teeth chattered!

"Finally the sun came up. Slowly the man turned around. And who do you think was holding him?"

Tomás smiled and said, "A thorny tree."

Papá Grande laughed. "Tomás, you know all my stories," he said. "There are many more in the library. You are big enough to go by yourself. Then you can teach us new stories."

The next morning Tomás walked downtown. He looked at the big library. Its tall windows were like eyes glaring at him. Tomás walked around and around the big building. He saw children coming out carrying books. Slowly he started climbing up, up the steps. He counted them to himself in Spanish. *Uno, dos, tres, cuatro . . .* His mouth felt full of cotton.

Tomás stood in front of the library doors. He pressed his nose against the glass and peeked in. The library was huge!

A hand tapped his shoulder. Tomás jumped. A tall lady looked down at him. "It's a hot day," she said. "Come inside and have a drink of water. What's your name?" she asked.

"Tomás," he said.

"Come, Tomás," she said.

Inside it was cool. Tomás had never seen so many books. The lady watched him. "Come," she said again, leading him to a drinking fountain. "First some water. Then I will bring books to this table for you. What would you like to read about?"

"Tigers. Dinosaurs," said Tomás.

Tomás drank the cold water. He looked at the tall ceiling. He looked at all the books around the room. He watched the lady take some books from the shelves and bring them to the table. "This chair is for you, Tomás," she said. Tomás sat down. Then very carefully he took a book from the pile and opened it.

Tomás saw dinosaurs bending their long necks to lap shiny water. He heard the cries of a wild snakebird. He felt the warm neck of the dinosaur as he held on tight for a ride. Tomás forgot about the library lady. He forgot about Iowa and Texas.

"Tomás, Tomás," said the library lady softly. Tomás looked around. The library was empty. The sun was setting.

The library lady looked at Tomás for a long time. She said, "Tomás, would you like to borrow two library books? I will check them out in my name."

Tomás walked out of the library carrying his books. He ran home, eager to show the new stories to his family.

Papá Grande looked at the library books. "Read to me," he said to Tomás. First Tomás showed him the pictures. He pointed to the tiger. *"¡Qué tigre tan grande!"* Tomás said first in Spanish and then in English, "What a big tiger!"

"Read to me in English," said Papá Grande. Tomás read about tiger eyes shining brightly in the jungle at night. He roared like a huge tiger. Papá, Mamá, and Enrique laughed. They came and sat near him to hear his story.

Some days Tomás went with his parents to the
town dump. They looked for pieces of iron to sell.
Enrique looked for toys. Tomás looked for books.
He would put the books in the sun to bake away
the smell.

All summer, whenever he could, Tomás went to
the library. The library lady would say, "First a
drink of water and then some new books, Tomás."

On quiet days the library lady said, "Come to my desk and read to me, Tomás." Then she would say, "Please teach me some new words in Spanish."

Tomás would smile. He liked being the teacher. The library lady pointed to a book. "Book is *libro*," said Tomás.

"*Libro*," said the library lady.

"*Pájaro*," said Tomás, flapping his arms.

The library lady laughed. "Bird," she said.

On days when the library was busy, Tomás read to himself. He'd look at the pictures for a long time. He smelled the smoke at an Indian camp. He rode a black horse across a hot, dusty desert. And in the evenings he would read the stories to Mamá, Papá, Papá Grande, and Enrique.

One August afternoon Tomás brought Papá Grande to the library.

The library lady said, *"Buenas tardes, señor."* Tomás smiled. He had taught the library lady how to say "Good afternoon, sir" in Spanish.

"Buenas tardes, señora," Papá Grande replied.

Softly Tomás said, "I have a sad word to teach you today. The word is *adiós*. It means good-bye."

Tomás was going back to Texas. He would miss this quiet place, the cool water, the many books. He would miss the library lady.

"My mother sent this to thank you," said Tomás, handing her a small package. "It is *pan dulce*, sweet bread. My mother makes the best *pan dulce* in Texas."

The library lady said, "How nice. How very nice. *Gracias*, Tomás. Thank you." She gave Tomás a big hug.

301

That night, bumping along again in the tired old car, Tomás held a shiny new book, a present from the library lady. Papá Grande smiled and said, "More stories for the new storyteller."

Tomás closed his eyes. He saw the dinosaurs drinking cool water long ago. He heard the cry of the wild snakebird. He felt the warm neck of the dinosaur as he held on tight for a bumpy ride.

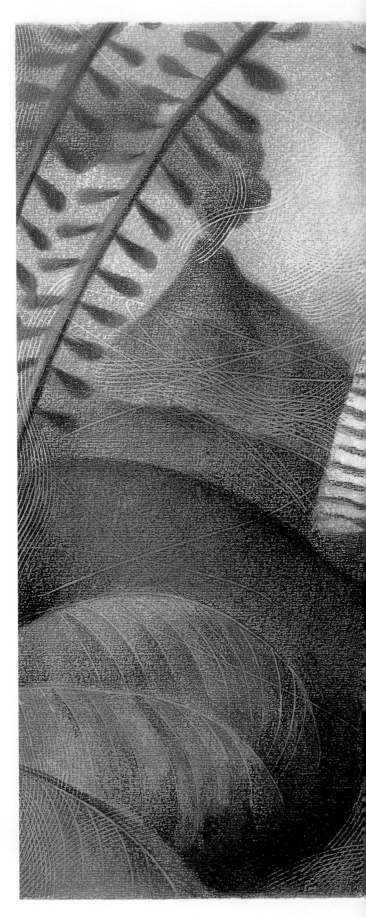

305

Story Questions & Activities

1 Why do Tomás and his family go back and forth between Texas and Iowa?

2 Why does Tomás go to the library?

3 How do you think Tomás feels about learning?

4 What is this story mainly about?

5 How do you think reading changed the lives of both Tomás and Grandma from "The Wednesday Surprise?"

Write an Adventure Story

Write a story about yourself that takes place in a different land. Maybe it's under water, on the moon, or in the rain forest. Who do you meet there? What happens? Make sure you include a beginning, middle, and end.

Make a Book Mark

It is important to take care of library books. One way is to make a book mark to hold your place. Fold a rectangle of waxed paper in half. Press leaves or flowers between the halves. Punch a hole in the top and string yarn or ribbon through it.

Share a Story

Tomás and his grandfather enjoy sharing stories. What is your favorite story? Share it with the class. You can read the story aloud, tell about what happens in the story, or act out your favorite part.

Find Out More

Tomás learns how wonderful libraries can be. Find out more about your local library. When was it built? How many books does it have? Besides books, what else can you find in the library?

Read a Library Floor Plan

Tomás spends a lot of time at a library.
A floor plan can help you find what you're
looking for in the library.

Library Floor Plan

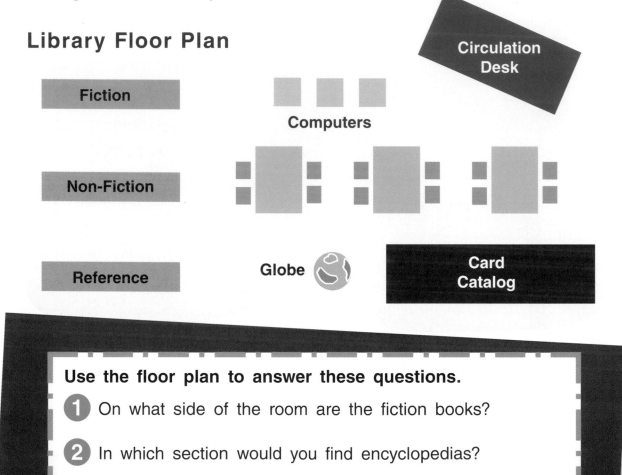

Use the floor plan to answer these questions.

1 On what side of the room are the fiction books?

2 In which section would you find encyclopedias?

3 Where would you go to check a book out?

4 Suppose six people want to use computers. How many people have to wait?

5 What books are closest to the reference books? What kind of books are these?

TEST POWER

Reading a story carefully will make it easier to answer the questions.

DIRECTIONS:

Read the story. Then read each question about the story.

SAMPLE

Special Delivery

There are lots of people who work at the post office. They help us send and get letters. These are very important jobs.

Some people at the post office sort the mail. First, they read the address on the envelope. Then, they put the envelope in the bag that goes to the right place. A different bag goes to each city. Some bags go by truck. Some bags go by airplane. New bags arrive every day from other places. These bags are full of letters that need to be delivered.

Other people at the post office deliver the mail. They are the letter carriers. They carry the letters from the post office to your house. Everyone likes to get mail. That is why the people at the post office are so important.

1 Which general statement can you make from this story?
- ○ Many people get their mail on Tuesdays.
- ○ It takes many people to make sure mail gets to the right place.
- ○ Most letter carriers fly planes.
- ○ Most mail has stamps on it.

2 In this story, some mail travels by—
- ○ bus
- ○ boat
- ○ airplane
- ○ train

Little Sister

My little sister follows me
　　Around both night and day,
She tugs my coat and won't let me go,
　　Until I stop and play.
If I do something secret,
　　My sister wants to know.
And if my friends invite me out,
　　She always wants to go.
You might think I'm angry,
　　You might think I'm mad,
But little sister is the best pal
　　That I ever had.

BY *K*ATHLEEN M. MULDOON
Illustrated by Linda Shute

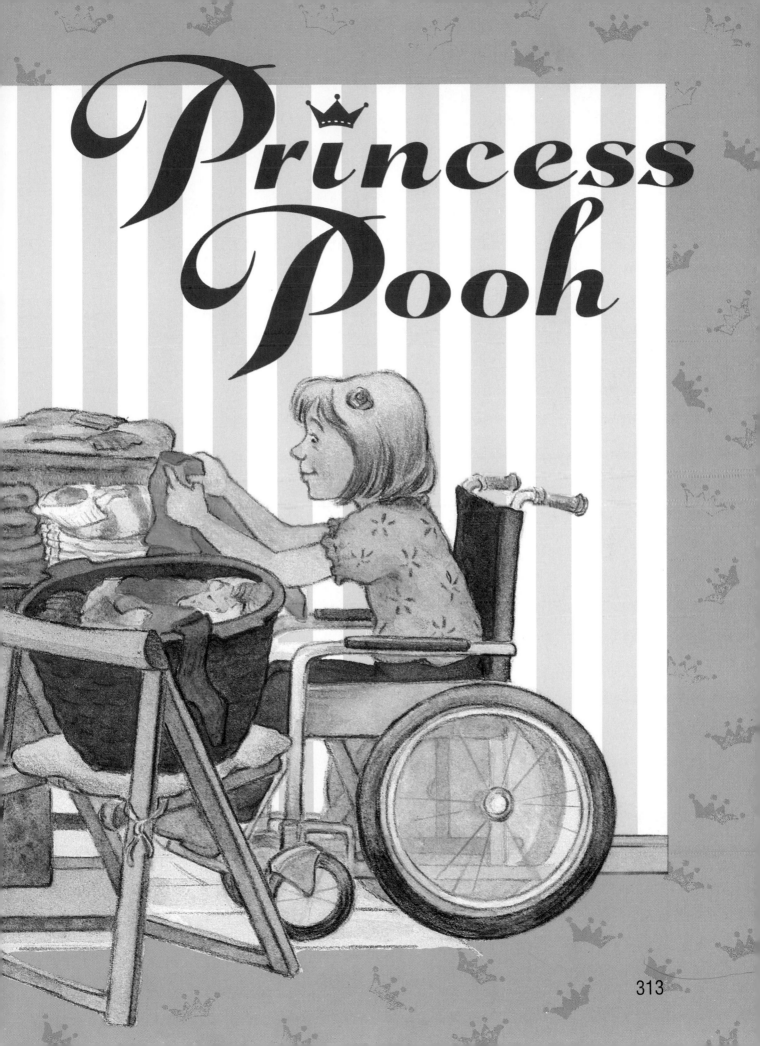

Princess Pooh

$\mathcal{M}$y big sister is ten years old. Her name is Penelope Marie Piper, but everyone calls her Penny. Everyone except me. I, Patty Jean Piper, call her Princess Pooh. No one knows I call her that, but it's the perfect name for her. All day she just sits on her throne with wheels and tells everybody in the whole world what to do.

Mrs. Meadows
COOKIES

When we go shopping at the mall, Princess Pooh rides on her throne while Dad wheels her around. She smiles and waves like she's some kind of movie star. Mom carries the Princess's crutches and I, Patty Jean the Servant, carry packages. Sometimes there are so many I look like a box with legs.

Everyone loves the Princess. Grandma and Grandpop and all the aunts and uncles and cousins in our family hug her and say how sweet and wonderful she is. Then they look at me and say I am growing like a weed. That's the way it has been for a million years. The Princess is a flower. I, plain old Patty Jean, am a weed.

Once we went to a carnival. Princess Pooh
watched me ride a hundred times on the roller
coaster. It was fun, but it would have been better
with a friend. I almost wished the Princess could
ride with me. Then I tried to win a pink stuffed
poodle. I spent all my allowance and threw a
thousand balls, but I couldn't knock down the
bottles. When we left, the man handed Princess
Pooh a yellow stuffed poodle with a diamond
collar! That's how it is. Everyone gives her things.

My school is a hundred years old. It is so far from my house I have to ride for hours on a school bus to get there. Princess Pooh goes to the new school right across the street. She can wheel herself there in one second.

If it rains, Dad carries her and her throne to his car and gives her a one-second ride. I, Patty Jean, wear an icky yellow raincoat and stand in mud puddles, waiting for the bus.

Saturday is chore day. Mom mows the lawn. Dad washes clothes and cleans the garage. Then he brings the clean clothes to the Princess, and she folds them into piles on the table. I, Patty Jean the Maid, clean the bathroom.

One Saturday, Mom asked me to fold clothes because Princess Pooh had therapy. I sat at the table pretending I was the Princess. I folded the clothes very fast and put them in perfect stacks. When the Princess came home, I waited for Mom to tell her to clean the bathroom. But Mom put her right to bed because she was tired. So I, exhausted Patty Jean, had to clean the bathroom, too.

It is summer now. All my friends have gone to camp—everyone except me. Mom says there's no money to send me to camp because the Princess got new braces for her legs.

Princess Pooh doesn't need them anyway because
all she does is sit. She only takes little tiny walks,
like when she has to go to the bathroom at a
restaurant and her wheelchair won't fit through
the door. Mom says she walks at therapy, too, but
I've never seen her do it.

After dinner I go outside. The Princess is in
the hammock reading a book.

"Do you want to make a puppet show?" I ask.

"No, thanks," she says in her princess voice.
"I'm going to read lots of books so I can win a
prize in the summer reading program."

I don't feel like reading, but I get a book anyway and look at the pictures. I am finished in one minute.

"This book is boring," I say. "Let's play with puppets now." The Princess doesn't answer. I look over at the hammock—there she is, asleep.

Behind the tree is the throne. Seeing it empty gives me the best idea anyone in the whole world has ever had. Today I, Patty Jean, will be the Princess!

I sit on the throne. It is covered with cushions and feels like a cloud.

"I will rest on my golden throne for the whole evening," I say. I imagine all the people in my kingdom, looking at me and loving their beautiful new princess.

The throne is hard to wheel on the grass, so I get up and pull it to the front yard. "Now I will spend *every minute* on the throne," I say.

I decide to ride to the Princess's school. There is a nice, steep little hill on the grass near the sidewalk. Maybe it would be fun to ride down it. I sit down and give the throne a good, hard push.

PLOP! The throne dumps me out on the sidewalk and lands upside down on top of me. My knee has a tiny cut on it, but it doesn't hurt much. Still, I'm glad no one is around to laugh. I wonder if Princess Pooh ever fell when she was learning. I put the throne rightside up and get back on it. Then I ride to the corner. I go down the low place on the curb so I can cross the street.

When the light turns green, I push the wheels as fast as I can. I make it to the island in the middle, but then the light turns red again.

Cars and trucks and buses rush by. I cover my face so I will not see myself go SPLAT.

Finally, the traffic stops and the light is green again. I finish crossing the street. I push the throne up the low place at the crosswalk. It is hard to go uphill, but I do it. I wheel down the sidewalk. I've been pushing so hard I feel like both my arms are broken.

Some grown-ups are walking toward me. They look at me and my throne, and then they turn away fast, like I do when I'm watching a scary movie. Does this happen to Princess Pooh?

Some boys are playing on the sidewalk and will not move out of my way. "Why don't you go over me, Wheel Legs?" says one of them. All his friends laugh. "I'll beat you up!" I yell, but they just laugh some more and run away.

I see an ice-cream truck on the school playground. Lots of big kids are crowded around it. I make a shortcut across the baseball field, but by the time I get there and take some money out of my pocket, the worst thing in the world has happened. Great big raindrops have started falling over everything! SLAM goes the window on the truck. The children squeal and run away. The man drives off and I'm alone on my wet throne.

The rain comes faster and faster. I think about running home, too, but I can't leave the throne out in the rain. Besides, I am still the Princess. I'm spending every minute on my throne, even if I do get wet! So I push harder and harder. When I get back to the baseball field, I can see it's a muddy mess. The wheels of the throne sink down, down, down. They stop turning. My hands are covered with mud. I jump off the throne, and my new sandals sink, too. My feet go with them. By the time I pull the throne out, I am wetter and colder than I have ever been in my whole life. I, Princess Patty Jean, am a royal mess. It is definitely time to quit sitting on the throne.

The rain stops. Across the
street there is a rainbow. I notice
Dad standing in our front yard.
He is calling and calling, but the
cars and trucks are so noisy I
can't hear him. Mom is walking up
the street, looking around. I drag
the muddy throne across the rest
of the field to the sidewalk.

Then I cross the
    street. When Mom
    sees me, she runs
    and holds out her
    arms. Dad is
    right behind her.
    "I didn't mean to
    mess up the throne.
    I'm sorry," I say.
        "Throne?" says
    Mom. "Oh, the
    wheelchair. We thought
    you were lost!"
        "You weren't looking
    for the chair?" I say.
    "Patty Jean, we were
    looking for *you*." Mom hugs me
    some more. "You shouldn't have
    taken Penny's chair. But we're
    so glad you're back!"

Mom washes me in the bathtub and puts me to bed just like she does for Penny. After Dad and Mom say good-night and turn out the lights, I lie there thinking.

"Penny," I whisper. "Are you awake?"

"Uh-huh."

"Do you like walking better than sitting?"

"Well," she says, "walking makes me awful tired, but so does pushing my wheelchair.

I guess I like the wheelchair best because I can do things with my hands while I sit. When I use my crutches, I can't."

"How can you smile all the time when you're in that yucky chair?"

"It's not yucky," says Penny. "It takes me places I can't go if I just have my crutches."

That makes me think some more. "I'm sorry I took your chair," I say.

"That's all right. Just go to sleep now."

Story Questions & Activities

1 What is Penelope's "throne with wheels"?

2 Why does Patty Jean call her sister "Princess"?

3 What does Patty Jean learn about using a wheelchair?

4 What is this story mainly about?

5 Both Patty Jean and Lizzie from "The Best Friends Club" learn important lessons that help them see people differently. Describe how you think each character changed.

Write Penelope's Story

What if this story was told by Penelope instead of Patty Jean? Imagine that you are Penelope, and you are writing in your journal about what happened the day your sister took your wheelchair. Tell the story of the day from beginning to end, and include how you felt about it.

336

Find Information about Families

Patty Jean has one sister. How many children are in your family? How many children are in your classmates' families? Write the name of each child in your family on a card. Don't forget yourself! Put the cards into different piles. Make one pile for families with one child. Make another pile for families with two children. Make a different pile for every number.

A Special Event

Patty Jean and her family go to a carnival. What special event have you been to or would like to go to? Draw a picture of that event. Write the name of the event and three things that happen at this event.

Find Out More

The Special Olympics is an international sporting event for the physically challenged. Find out more about the Special Olympics. When did they start? What are the events?

STUDY SKILLS

Use an Encyclopedia

---

112   Hawking, Stephen   Hay

Hawking, Stephen William

(1942–   ) Stephen William Hawking is a British scientist. Hawking studies questions about the universe.

Stephen Hawking has a disease called ALS. He can't talk. He can only move a few muscles in his hands and face. But Hawking still is able to work. He uses a wheelchair, and a computer that talks for him. Besides studying science, he also works for the rights of disabled people.

Use the part of an encyclopedia page to answer the questions.

1 What volume would have this entry about Stephen Hawking? Explain.

2 What are the guide words on this page?

3 What is Stephen Hawking's disability?

4 How does he communicate?

5 What work besides science does Stephen Hawking do?

TEST POWER

DIRECTIONS:

Read the story. Then read each question about the story.

SAMPLE

Which One Will Win?

Every October there is a pumpkin contest. Many people enter their pumpkins in the contest. There are many kinds of pumpkins in the contest. Some are small. Some are big. Some are giant. When people enter the contest, this is what they must do. First, they must weigh their pumpkin. Next, they must measure the pumpkin at its fattest point. Then, they must show their pumpkins to the judges. The judges know everything about pumpkins. The judges look at each pumpkin. They look at its shape, its color, and its size. Then, they choose a winner. Every winner gets a medal. The best winner gets the gold medal.

1 What is the main idea of this story?
   ○ The best pumpkin is judged in many ways.
   ○ Growing pumpkins is easy.
   ○ My pumpkin is the best one.
   ○ Pumpkin pie tastes good.

2 Which is a general statement that you can make from this story?
   ○ Small pumpkins are best.
   ○ Judges consider many things when choosing a winner of a contest.
   ○ All pumpkins are giant.
   ○ Pumpkin contests can only happen in October.

Party Time

Change into your swimsuit,
   Get your flippers, follow me.
We're going to a party
   Underneath the deep, blue sea.
You're sure to have a nice time
   In this strange and fishy place,
Where crab and lobster crawl about
   And watch the seahorse race.
Have a slice of fishcake
   And a bit of seafood stew.
Then shake hands with the octopus,
   And say, "How do you do."

When asked how he came up with the idea for the story *Swimmy,* Leo Lionni said, "I was watching the minnows swimming around in the harbor one day. Standing by the water that day, I didn't have an idea for a book. But later, as I began writing the book, I realized seeing the fish gave me the idea and set the story off.

"For the art in this book, I used a lot of wet paint. To make the watery background, I put the paint on a piece of glass. Then I pressed paper onto the glass so it would pick up the paint. I used my hand to spread the paint. Then I lifted the paper off the glass, and it made a watery ocean for Swimmy and his friends. Then I cut up pieces of paper to make a collage. Swimmy and the little red fish were little rubber stamps."

Meet **Leo Lionni**

342

Swimmy

by Leo Lionni

A happy school of little fish lived in a corner of the sea somewhere. They were all red. Only one of them was as black as a mussel shell. He swam faster than his brothers and sisters. His name was Swimmy.

One bad day a tuna fish, swift, fierce and very
hungry, came darting through the waves. In one
gulp he swallowed all the little red fish.

Only Swimmy escaped. He swam away in the deep wet world. He was scared, lonely and very sad.

But the sea was full of wonderful creatures, and as he swam from marvel to marvel Swimmy was happy again.

He saw a medusa made of rainbow jelly. . .

a lobster, who walked about like a
water-moving machine . . .

strange fish, pulled by an invisible thread . . .

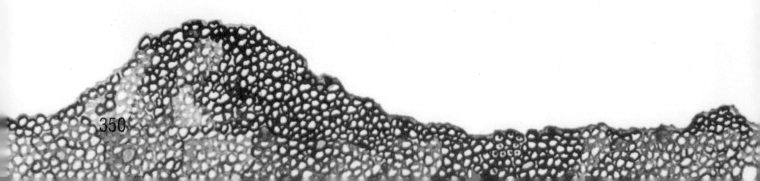

a forest of seaweeds growing from
sugar-candy rocks . . .

an eel whose tail was almost too
far away to remember . . .

and sea anemones, who looked
like pink palm trees swaying
in the wind.

353

Then, hidden in the dark shade of rocks and weeds, he saw a school of little fish, just like his own.

"Let's go and swim and play and SEE things!" he said happily.

"We can't," said the little red fish. "The big fish will eat us all."

"But you can't just lie there," said Swimmy. "We must THINK of something."

Swimmy thought and thought and thought. Then suddenly he said, "I have it! We are going to swim all together like the biggest fish in the sea!"

355

He taught them to swim close together, each in his own place, and when they had learned to swim like one giant fish, he said, "I'll be the eye."

And so they swam in the cool morning water and in the midday sun and chased the big fish away.

Story Questions & Activities

1. At the beginning of the story, what happens to the little red fish?

2. At the end of the story, why does the big fish get chased away?

3. What makes Swimmy a good leader?

4. What is this story about?

5. The animals in "The Bremen Town Musicians" and the fish in "Swimmy" have the same problem. What is it? How do they solve it?

Write a Fairy Tale

Write a fairy tale about a group of small animals, insects, or birds who have a problem. Can they be stronger together than alone? Show how they work together to solve their problem.

Hide and Seek

By pretending to be one large fish, Swimmy and his friends were able to hide themselves. Draw a picture that shows how another animal hides itself. Describe it.

Make a Pet Graph

"Swimmy" tells the story of a small fish. Have you ever had a fish as a pet? What kinds of pets do you and your classmates have? Find out what pets your classmates have. Count the total number of each kind of pet. Show your results in a bar graph.

Find Out More

Swimmy sees all kinds of animals in the sea. Find out about one animal that lives in the ocean. Write down three facts about that animal.

STUDY SKILLS

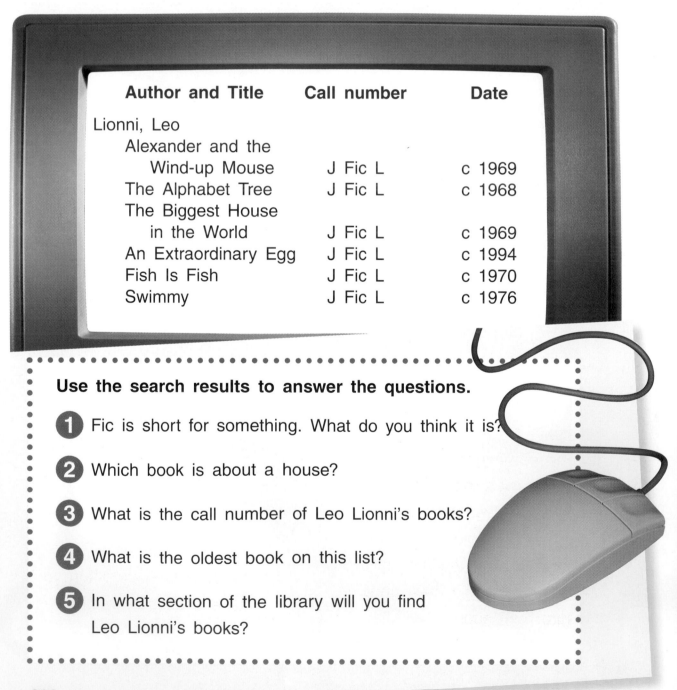

Do an Author Search at the Library

Here are the results of a search for books by Leo Lionni at a library.

Author and Title	Call number	Date
Lionni, Leo		
Alexander and the Wind-up Mouse	J Fic L	c 1969
The Alphabet Tree	J Fic L	c 1968
The Biggest House in the World	J Fic L	c 1969
An Extraordinary Egg	J Fic L	c 1994
Fish Is Fish	J Fic L	c 1970
Swimmy	J Fic L	c 1976

Use the search results to answer the questions.

1 Fic is short for something. What do you think it is?

2 Which book is about a house?

3 What is the call number of Leo Lionni's books?

4 What is the oldest book on this list?

5 In what section of the library will you find Leo Lionni's books?

Take your time reading the story, the questions, and the answers.

DIRECTIONS:

Read the story. Then read each question about the story.

SAMPLE

Going on a Treasure Hunt

Tammy invited Pat over for a treasure hunt. When Pat arrived, Tammy gave her a list of things to find. Pat was very excited, since she had never been on a treasure hunt before. Pat had to look for or find out:

a green leaf, a dog hair, a bug, a flower, Tammy's mother's birthday, and the cat's name.

When Pat found all of the things on her list, she called to Tammy. Tammy checked that everything was there. She told Pat that she had done a great job in a short time. Pat thanked Tammy for all of the fun and asked if they could have another treasure hunt soon.

1 Which of these is a general statement you can make from this story?
- ○ Finding bugs is an easy thing to do.
- ○ Spending time with a friend can be a lot of fun.
- ○ All friends like to look for things.
- ○ Most treasure hunts take a long time.

2 What is this story mostly about?
- ○ Tammy and Pat's treasure hunt
- ○ Pat's house
- ○ Tammy's mother
- ○ What to look for when you have a treasure hunt

The Plan

Here's the plan. My friend began it.
Plant a plant to save the planet.
Every village, every place
Needs some green. So just in case
Your town is turning brown and bland,
Plant a seed right in the land.
Watch your plant grow every day
And soon your friends will see the way
To turn your town from brown to WOW.
So plan to plant a plant right now!

TIME

FOR KIDS

The World's
Plants
Are in
DANGER

Where Are All the Flowers Going?

Be careful next time you think of picking a pretty wildflower. It may be in danger of disappearing forever. That's the bad news from the World Conservation Union. The group spent 20 years coming up with a list of plants in trouble. The list names about 34,000 types of plants, trees, bushes, and flowers. Some kinds of palm trees, roses, lilies, and wildflowers are on the list.

The rafflesia is the world's largest flower. It can be three feet across.

Wildflowers cover these California hills.

365

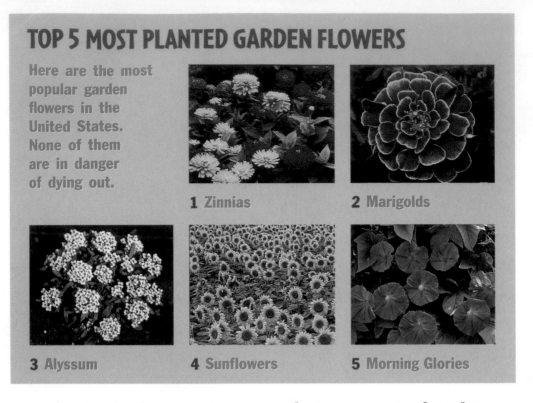

TOP 5 MOST PLANTED GARDEN FLOWERS

Here are the most popular garden flowers in the United States. None of them are in danger of dying out.

1 Zinnias

2 Marigolds

3 Alyssum

4 Sunflowers

5 Morning Glories

The Union's report warns that one out of eight types of plants in the world may die out. In the United States, nearly one out of three plants is in danger of disappearing. Many kinds of plants in danger can only be found in one part of the world. Some coral plants, for example, are found only in Chile.

Plants disappear when humans destroy the places where plants live. This problem can happen when people build new roads, factories, or homes. Plants and trees can also disappear as land is cleared for other uses.

Sometimes, plants from one part of the world are brought to another part of the world.

Plants die when rain forests are cleared.

DAVID MUENCH/CORBIS

**The saguaro cactus
is protected in Arizona.**

The new plants may crowd out other plants that have been in that spot for hundreds of years.

Why is it so important to save plants? "Plants clothe us, feed us, and provide us with most of our medicines," says David Brackett. He is with the World Conservation Union. Brackett warns that people must pay attention to the world's plants and help keep them safe. If we don't, some of nature's beauty may disappear forever.

PLEASE, DON'T PICK THE FLOWERS

About one out of every 10 kinds of U.S. wildflowers is in danger of disappearing. The U.S. doesn't want to lose these flowers. So it is against the law to pick wildflowers in U.S. parks and forests. In many states, it is against the law to pick wildflowers anywhere. These laws help save the flowers, so people will be able to enjoy them for years to come.

FIND OUT MORE
Visit our website:
www.mhschool.com/reading

*inter*NET
CONNECTION

Based on an article in *TIME FOR KIDS.*

Story Questions & Activities

1. What did the World Conservation Union make a list about?

2. Why does David Brackett think it is important to save plants?

3. Why have some states made it against the law to pick wildflowers?

4. What is the main idea of this selection?

5. What other plants and animals have you read about that might become extinct? How can people help save wildflowers? How can people help save other plants or animals?

Write a Story

Write a story about a plant that is in danger. Tell how it saves itself and its family, and how you might help it. Be sure the story has a beginning, a middle, and an end.

368

Create a Community Guide

Where are the green places in your community? List the places in your neighborhood where you can go to see and smell flowers and other plants. Include parks, flower stores, and plant stores. Tell a little about each place. You might want to draw a map to show where these places are.

Prepare a Speech

Prepare a speech giving some reasons why it is important to protect flowers and plants. Include ways that you could help protect endangered plants in your community.

Find Out More

Every state has a state flower. What is your state's flower? Why was it chosen? What does it look like? Is it an endangered plant?

369

STUDY SKILLS

Choose a Reference Source

Dictionary

flower 1. A plant grown for its brightly colored petals. The garden was full of red and yellow *flowers. Noun.* **2.** To produce flowers; blossom. Cherry trees *flower* in early spring. *Verb.*

   flow·er (flou´ər) *noun, plural* **flowers**; *verb* **flowered**, **flowering**.

Encyclopedia

flower A flower is a plant that has colorful blossoms. Examples of popular flowers are buttercups, dandelions, roses, tulips, and violets. There are hundreds of other garden flowers and wildflowers.

Nonfiction Book

How to Care for Your Flowers
by Daisy Littlefield

Telephone Directory

Flower Stores

Anne's Flowers.............525-6784
Flowers by Ellen..........490-3835
Mostly Orchids.............718-4049

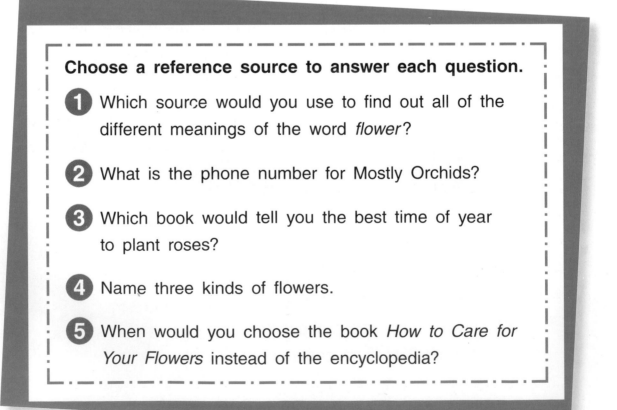

Choose a reference source to answer each question.

1 Which source would you use to find out all of the different meanings of the word *flower*?

2 What is the phone number for Mostly Orchids?

3 Which book would tell you the best time of year to plant roses?

4 Name three kinds of flowers.

5 When would you choose the book *How to Care for Your Flowers* instead of the encyclopedia?

Ask yourself the questions again, but use your own words.

DIRECTIONS:

Read the story. Then read each question about the story.

SAMPLE

Ron and Liz's Adventure

Ron and Liz and their mom went fishing. Liz carried the poles, and Ron carried the jar of worms. They all fished for a couple of hours. Ron caught a sunfish. His mother showed him how to carefully remove the hook so that the fish would not be hurt. Then, she gently put the fish back into the water. Ron watched it swim away. Liz thought that she had caught a fish, but it turned out to be weeds. Even though Liz was disappointed, she still laughed. After a while, they were all hungry for lunch. They carefully packed up their things and went home.

1 What is the main idea of this story?
   ○ Ron and Liz enjoy fishing with their mother.
   ○ Ron and Liz learned how to cook a fish.
   ○ Ron and Liz know where to go to catch fish.
   ○ Catching a bunch of weeds is disappointing.

2 What does Ron's mother do with the fish that Ron caught?
   ○ Takes it home to put in the fish pond.
   ○ Takes the hook out and puts it back in the water.
   ○ Shows the fish's tail to Ron and Liz.
   ○ Takes a picture of it.

IF YOU EVER MEET A WHALE

Traditional Rhyme

If you ever, ever, ever, ever,
ever meet a whale,
You must never, never, never, never
grab him by his tail.
If you ever, ever, ever, ever
grab him by his tail—
You will never, never, never, never
meet another whale.

373

Reading for

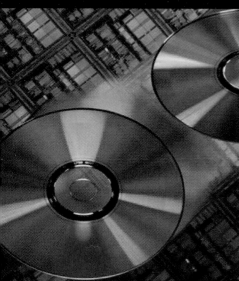

You get information from many sources such as television, newspapers, advertisements, and the Internet. In school, textbooks bring you information about different subjects. In this section, you will learn strategies to help you understand and use the many kinds of information that are a part of your everyday life.

Information

Contents

A science book tells facts about things and ideas. Thinking about how things are alike and different helps you to understand them. When you compare two things, you look at how they are alike. You also look at how they are different. As you read, you may want to use a chart like the one below to help you.

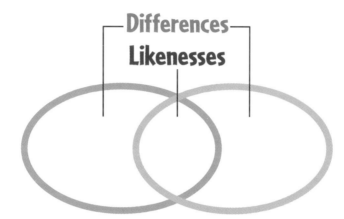

Differences
Likenesses

Make Comparisons

1. **Choose two things** to compare. Look at pictures, titles, and captions for ideas.

2. **Compare two things.** As you read, find details that tell how the things are alike.

3. **Look for differences.** Find details that tell how the things are different.

4. **Organize** the information. List all the ways in which the two things are alike. Then list the differences.

Ponds and Streams

Vocabulary

| pond | habitat |
| fresh water | stream |

What lives in a pond?

A **pond** is a **fresh water habitat**. Fresh water has little or no salt in it. Like water in a pool, pond water stays in one place. Plants grow in and around the pond. Some plants even float on the water.

Many pond fish eat water plants and insects. Birds make nests with pond grass. Beavers build homes with branches from nearby trees.

What lives in a stream?

A **stream** is a fresh water habitat with moving water. Salmon swim in streams. Sometimes they swim against the flow of the water to find a place to lay eggs.

①

Choose.
I'll scan this page. Can titles help me choose two things to compare?

②

Compare.
Ponds and streams are both fresh water habitats.

③

Look for differences.
Unlike ponds, streams have moving water.

④

Organize.
I'll list the ways ponds and streams are alike and different.

Where Plants and Animals Live

Living in the mountains is not easy! The weather is cold. The ground is rocky. Why do you think this mountain goat makes its home here? Talk about what it needs to live.

Science Skill

When you **communicate**, you talk, write, or draw to share your ideas.

Explore Activity

Where do animals live?

What you need

animal pictures cut from magazines

drawings or pictures of places animals live

What to do:

1 Put the pictures of animals in one group. Put the pictures of places animals live in another group.

2 Match each animal with the place where it lives.

3 **Communicate** why you matched the cards the way you did.

What is a habitat?

A **habitat** is a place where plants and animals can meet their needs. Different plants and animals live in different habitats. Habitats can be on land or in the water. The animals in these pictures live near water. This is where they can find what they need to live.

water strider

otter

alligator

kingfisher

The animals in a habitat need plants. They also need each other. Some animals use plants for shelter. Many eat plants. Some animals eat other animals. This bird lives near water because it eats the fish that live there.

▷ **How are these animals meeting their needs?**

Review Questions

1. What is a habitat?

2. What do animals get from their habitats?

3. How does a science book help us learn about plants and animals?

catfish

Learning to check the information you read is an important skill. Facts in different books or sources may disagree with each other. Information may be out of date. The questions below can help you check your facts.

It says that blue whales can grow to 100 feet (30 meters) long. I can check this fact out in the encyclopedia!

Check Facts

1 **Does the information make sense?** Does it fit with what you already know?

2 **Where can I check?** Look in an encyclopedia or a book on the topic.

3 **Whom can I ask?** Ask an adult at school or at home. This person might help you find out if a fact is correct.

4 **Is there newer information?** It is important to use information that is up-to-date.

Does it make sense? I know that whales are very big.

 Where can I check? I could look in an encyclopedia.

3 **Whom can I ask?** I could ask the librarian.

4 **Is there newer information?** Is this still true?

Nonfiction Book

BLUE WHALES

The blue whale is probably the largest animal that has ever lived. Its body is bigger than the largest dinosaur. It makes a sound so loud that it can be heard 100 miles (160 km) away.

Blue whales look like large fish, but they are not. Blue whales keep a constant body temperature, the same as you do. Fish do not. Blue whales have lungs and cannot breathe underwater. Fish use their gills to breathe underwater.

Most blue whales live in Earth's southern oceans. Laws protect these whales from being hunted. Even so, only a small number remain.

Encyclopedia

Dinosaurs

Dinosaur bones have been found all over the world. Scientists who study the bones have learned that some dinosaurs ate meat and others ate plants. Some dinosaurs walked on two legs, while others walked on four legs.

Some scientists think dinosaurs died when a huge meteor crashed into Earth. It caused dust to fly into the air and block the sunlight. Without sun, plants could not grow. The dinosaurs that ate plants died. Then, dinosaurs that ate meat had nothing to eat. They died, too.

Magazine

Can You Dig It?

New dinosaur fossils were discovered in China in 1996. The fossils included feathers that look like those on a bird. Some scientists think that the first birds were dinosaurs.

Meat-eating dinosaurs and birds have some of the same kinds of bones. These dinosaurs also have feet like birds. Three toes point forward. One toe points backward.

Scientists will go on studying these fossils and bones. Thanks to their work, we may someday know for sure if birds came from dinosaurs.

Review Questions

1. Name two facts from the encyclopedia entry or magazine article that you could check in another source.

2. Why might ideas about dinosaurs change over time?

3. Why is it important to look for newer information?

E-mail, or electronic mail, lets you write and send letters on the computer. Your reader will get the letter just minutes after you send it. You can write to someone next door or many miles away.

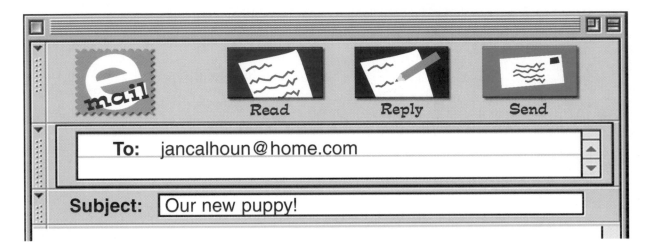

Read   Reply   Send

To: jancalhoun@home.com

Subject: Our new puppy!

Use a Computer

Our New Puppy!

1 **Type the e-mail address** in the box marked **To:**

2 **Type what your letter is about** in the **Subject** box.

3 **Type your letter** on the screen.

4 **Reread your letter.** Does it make sense? Did you leave out any words?

5 **Click on Send** to "mail" your letter.

Writing an E-mail

1 Type the e-mail address. This tells who the letter will go to. I'm sending this to Jan Calhoun.

2 Type the subject. My letter is about our new puppy.

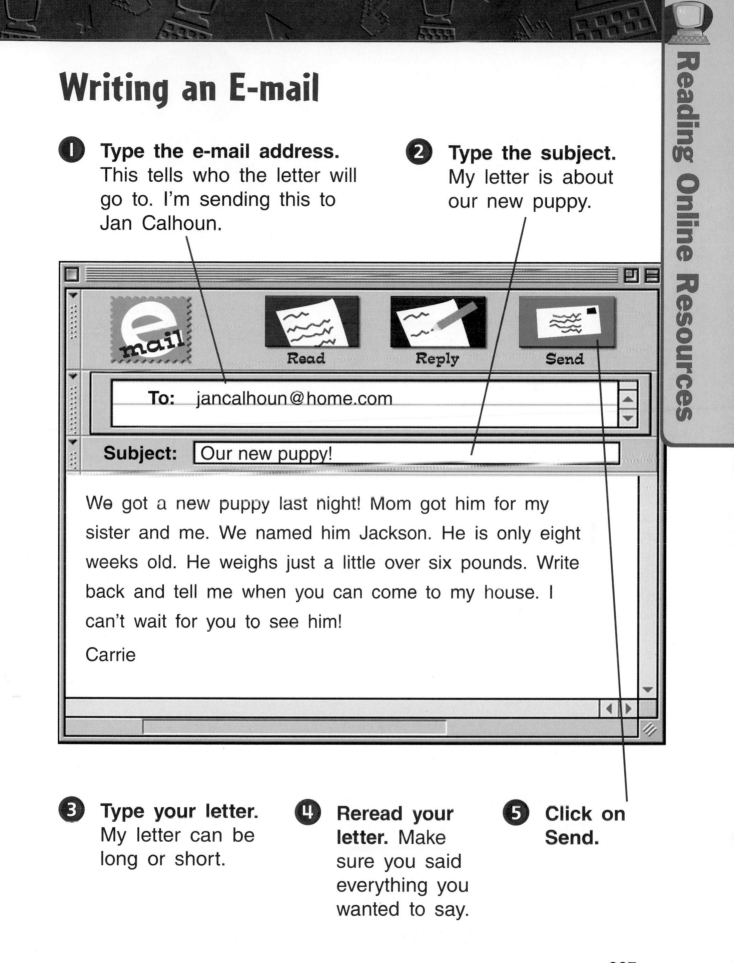

To: jancalhoun@home.com

Subject: Our new puppy!

We got a new puppy last night! Mom got him for my sister and me. We named him Jackson. He is only eight weeks old. He weighs just a little over six pounds. Write back and tell me when you can come to my house. I can't wait for you to see him!

Carrie

3 Type your letter. My letter can be long or short.

4 Reread your letter. Make sure you said everything you wanted to say.

5 Click on Send.

E-mail to a Friend

Kevin wrote an e-mail to his friend Kesha. He wanted to tell her about a book that he had read.

Read   **Reply**   **Send**

To: keshaallen@school.com

Subject: Great book!

I just read an exciting book! You would like it, too. In the story, a cat lives with a boy in his house. She jumps out a window and runs away. The boy looks everywhere for her but cannot find her.

It has a great ending. The cat comes back and they are both happy. You should read the book!

Kevin

The Friend's Reply

Here is Kesha's answer to Kevin. To write back to him, first she clicked on the **Reply** button. Then she wrote her letter, reread it, and sent it.

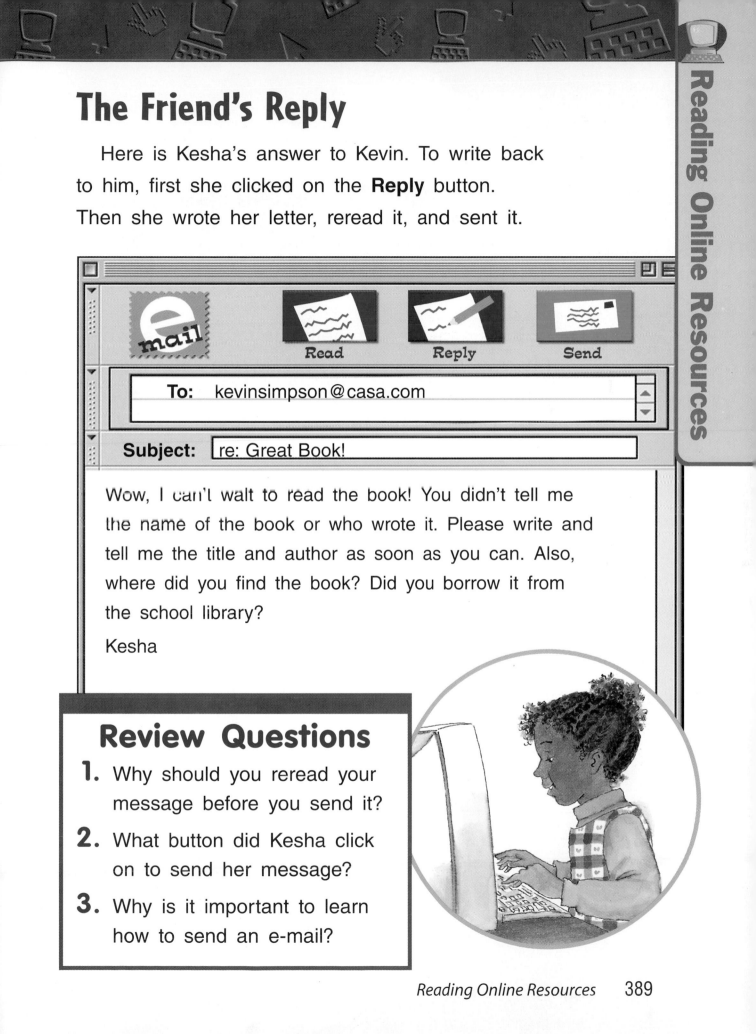

Read   Reply   Send

To: kevinsimpson@casa.com

Subject: re: Great Book!

Wow, I can't wait to read the book! You didn't tell me the name of the book or who wrote it. Please write and tell me the title and author as soon as you can. Also, where did you find the book? Did you borrow it from the school library?

Kesha

Review Questions

1. Why should you reread your message before you send it?

2. What button did Kesha click on to send her message?

3. Why is it important to learn how to send an e-mail?

Glossary

This glossary can help you find the **meanings** of words. If you see a word that you don't understand, try to find it in the glossary. The words are in **alphabetical order. Guide words** at the top of each page tell you the first and last words on the page.

The glossary shows you how to say the words, too. Each word is divided into **syllables.** Next, a special respelling, called the **pronunciation,** spells the word just the way it sounds.

The glossary also shows you **synonyms** for words. A **synonym** is a word that can be used for another word. A synonym for *field* is *grass.*

Sample Entry

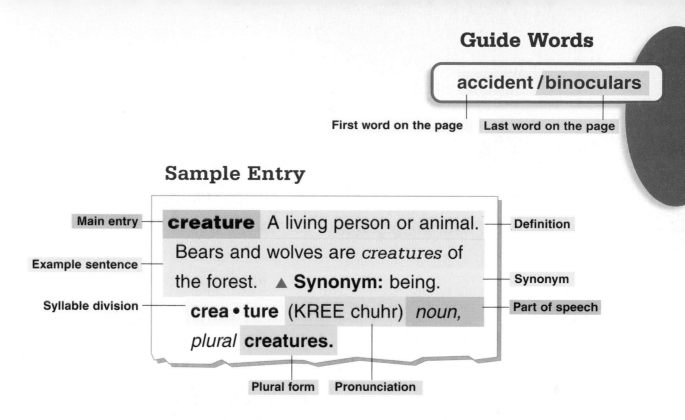

Main entry — **creature** A living person or animal. — Definition

Example sentence — Bears and wolves are *creatures* of the forest. ▲ **Synonym:** being. — Synonym

Syllable division — **crea•ture** (KREE chuhr) *noun,* — Part of speech

plural **creatures.**

Plural form   Pronunciation

Use the **Pronunciation Key** below to find examples for the sounds you see in the **pronunciation** spellings.

Phonetic Spelling	Examples	Phonetic Spelling	Examples
a	cat	oh	go, home
ah	father	aw	saw, fall
ay	late, day	or	more, four
air	there, hair	oo	too, do
b	bit, rabbit	oy	toy
ch	chin	ow	out, cow
d	dog	p	pig
e	met	r	run, carry
ee	he, see	s	song, mess
f	fine, off	sh	shout, fish
g	go, bag, bigger	t	ten, better
h	hat	th	thin
hw	wheel	thh	them
ih	sit	u	sun
ī	fine, tiger, my	u̇	look, should
ihr	near, deer, here	yoo	music, new
j	jump, page	ur	turn, learn
k	cat, back	v	very, of
l	line, hill	w	we
m	mine, hammer	y	yes
n	nice, funny	z	has, zoo
ng	sing	zh	treasure, division
o	top	uh	about, happen, lemon

Aa

accident Something unlucky that happens without warning. There were many *accidents* the day of the snowstorm.

▲ **Synonym:** mishap.

ac•ci•dent (AK sih duhnt) *noun, plural* **accidents.**

afraid Feeling fear; frightened. There is no reason to be *afraid* of bats.

▲ **Synonym:** scared.

a•fraid (uh FRAYD) *adjective.*

Alamo (AL uh moh)

alyssum A plant of the mustard family that bears small white or yellow flowers.

a•lys•sum (uh LIHS um) *noun, plural* **alyssum.**

audience A group of people gathered to hear and see something. My family was in the *audience* to watch my school play

▲ **Synonyms:** spectators, listeners.

au•di•ence (AW dee uhns) *noun, plural* **audiences.**

auditorium A large room or building where people can gather. The concert will be in the school *auditorium.*

au•di•to•ri•um (aw dih TOR ee uhm) *noun, plural* **auditoriums.**

Bb

binoculars A device that makes distant objects look larger and closer, made up of two small telescopes joined together. We needed *binoculars* to see the ship on the horizon.
  bi•noc•u•lars (buh NAHK yoo luhrz) *plural noun.*

borrow To take something to use for a while. Hector let me *borrow* his roller skates.
  bor•row (BAHR oh) *verb,* **borrowed, borrowing.**

brachiopod Any of a large group of sea animals having a shell with a top and bottom half. We saw several different *brachiopods* while scuba diving.
  bra•chi•o•pod (BRAY kee uh pahd) *noun, plural* **brachiopods.**

brave Having courage. The *brave* lifeguard jumped into the water to save the child.
  brave (BRAYV) *adjective,* **braver, bravest.**

bravo Well done! Good! Excellent! The grateful audience clapped and cried *"Bravo!"*
  bra•vo (BRAH voh) *interjection, plural* **bravos** or **bravoes.**

breath Air drawn into and forced out of the lungs; respiration. The doctor asked me to take a big *breath.*
  breath (BRETH) *noun, plural* **breaths.**

Buenas noches Spanish for "good night." (BWAY nuhs NOH chez)

393

bulletin board A board for putting up notices, announcements, and pictures. She pinned the advertisement on the *bulletin board*.
> **bul•le•tin board** (BÛL ih tihn bord) *noun, plural* **bulletin boards.**

bumblebee A large bee with a thick, hairy body. Most *bumblebees* have yellow and black stripes.
> **bum•ble•bee** (BUHM buhl bee) *noun, plural* **bumblebees.**

burrito A Mexican food made of a tortilla wrapped around a filling. We had a choice of *burritos* or pizza for dinner.
> **bur•ri•to** (bur EE toh) *noun, plural* **burritos.**

bury To cover up; hide. The letter was *buried* in a pile of papers.
> ▲ **Synonyms:** conceal, hide.
> **bur•y** (BER ee) *verb,* **buried, burying.**

chance 1. A turn to do something. Each child will have a *chance* to ride the pony. **2.** The possibility that something might happen. There is a *chance* that it may snow tomorrow.
> ▲ **Synonym:** opportunity.
> **chance** (CHANS) *noun, plural* **chances.**

change 1. To make or become different. I will *change* the way I sign my name. *Verb.* **2.** The money that is given back when something costs less than the amount paid for it. I gave the ice cream man a dollar and got back twenty cents in *change*. *Noun.*
> **change** (CHAYNJ) *verb,* **changed, changing;** *noun, plural* **changes.**

cheer The shout you make to give someone hope or courage.
cheer (CHIHR) *noun*, *plural* **cheers.**

chocolate A food used in making sweet things to eat. Billy unwrapped the bar of *chocolate.*
choc•o•late (CHAWK liht) *noun, plural* **chocolates.**

clear 1. To remove things from. I *cleared* the dishes after supper. *Verb.* **2.** Free from anything that darkens; bright. The sky is *clear* today. *Adjective.*
clear (KLIHR) *verb*, **cleared, clearing;** *adjective*, **clearer, clearest.**

clothes Things worn to cover the body. Coats, dresses, pants, and jackets are kinds of *clothes.*
▲ **Synonym:** clothing.
clothes (KLOHZ *or* KLOHTHHZ) *plural noun.*

coach A person who trains athletes. The *coach* made the team practice every day.
▲ **Synonym:** trainer.
coach (KOHCH) *noun, plural* **coaches.**

collide To crash against each other. The two players *collided* as they chased the ball.
col•lide (kuh LĪD) *verb*, **collided, colliding.**

colony 1. A group of animals of the same kind that live together. Ants live in *colonies.* **2.** A territory ruled by another country. The British *colonies* became the United States.
col•ony (KOL uh nee) *noun, plural* **colonies.**

395

coral 1. A hard, stony substance found in tropical seas. We saw huge pieces of *coral* while scuba-diving. *Noun.* **2.** A pinkish red color. Her nail polish matched her *coral* sweater. *Adjective.*
> **cor•al** (KOR uhl) *noun, plural* **corals.**

Costa Rica A country in Central America. (KOH stuh REE kuh)

cousin The child of an aunt or uncle. My *cousin* and I have the same grandfather.
> **cou•sin** (KUZ ihn) *noun, plural* **cousins.**

cover 1. To put something on or over. *Cover* your head with a hat in cold weather. *Verb.* **2.** Something that is put on or over something else. The *cover* will keep the juice from spilling. *Noun.*
> **cov•er** (KUV uhr) *verb,* **covered, covering;** *noun, plural* **covers.**

creature A living person or animal. Bears and wolves are *creatures* of the forest.
> ▲ **Synonym:** being.
> **crea•ture** (KREE chuhr) *noun, plural* **creatures.**

crinoid Any of a group of colorful, flower-shaped saltwater animals. Crinoids are usually found in deep tropical waters. The glass-bottom boat let us see the colorful *crinoids* and coral on the ocean floor.
> **cri•noid** (KRĪ noyd) *noun, plural* **crinoids.**

Cristobal (KRIHS tuh bahl)

crocodile A long animal with short legs, thick, scaly skin, and a long, powerful tail. *Crocodiles* have longer heads than alligators.
   croc•o•dile (KROK uh dīl) *noun, plural* **crocodiles.**

crop Plants grown to be used as food. I grew my own *crop* of tomatoes in our garden.
   crop (KROP) *noun, plural* **crops.**

crowd 1. To put or force too many people or things into too small a space. My cousin *crowded* the shelf with books. *Verb.* **2.** A large group of people in one place. The *crowd* waited for the game to start. *Noun.*
   ▲ **Synonyms:** swarm, flock, assembly.
   crowd (KROWD) *verb,* **crowded, crowding;** *noun, plural* **crowds.**

darkness Little or no light. *Darkness* comes earlier in the winter.
   dark•ness (DAHRK nihss) *noun.*

daughter The female child of a mother and a father. Claire is the *daughter* of her mother and father. Claire's mother is the *daughter* of Claire's grandmother and grandfather.
   daugh•ter (DAW tuhr) *noun, plural* **daughters.**

desert A hot, dry, sandy area of land. It can be hard to find water in the *desert.*
   des•ert (DEZ uhrt) *noun, plural* **deserts.**

397

disappear 1. To go out of sight. We watched the moon *disappear* behind the clouds. 2. To become extinct. The dinosaurs *disappeared* from the earth millions of years ago.

> **dis•ap•pear** (dihs uh PIHR) *verb,* **disappeared, disappearing.**

disturb To break in on; to interrupt. The telephone call *disturbed* everyone's sleep.

> ▲ **Synonym:** bother.
> **dis•turb** (dihs TURB) *verb,* **disturbed, disturbing.**

dive To go into the water with your head first. When Maria and Carlos took swimming lessons, they learned how to *dive.*

> ▲ **Synonym:** plunge.
> **dive** (DĪV) *verb,* **dived** or **dove, dived, diving.**

398

dribble To move a ball along by bouncing or kicking it. Players *dribble* the basketball.

> **drib•ble** (DRIHB uhl) *verb,* **dribbled, dribbling.**

Ee

echolocation A method of determining the location of objects by bouncing sound waves off the objects.

> **ech•o•lo•ca•tion** (EK oh loh KAY shun) *noun.*

eel A long, thin fish that looks like a snake. The *eel* darted swiftly through the water.

> **eel** (EEL) *noun, plural* **eels.**

endanger To threaten with becoming extinct. Pollution *endangers* many species.

> **en•dan•ger** (en DAYN juhr) *verb,* **endangered, endangering.**

envy 1. A feeling of disliking or desiring another person's good luck or belongings. I felt *envy* for your new toy. *Noun.*
▲ **Synonym:** jealousy.
2. To feel envy toward. Everyone in our class *envies* you because of your good grades. *Verb.*
en•vy (EN vee) *noun, plural* **envies;** *verb,* **envied, envying.**

escape To get away from something. People knew a storm was coming and could *escape* before it started.
es•cape (es KAYP) *verb,* **escaped, escaping.**

evening The time of day when it starts to get dark, between afternoon and night. We eat dinner at 6 o'clock in the *evening.*
▲ **Synonyms:** dusk, nightfall, twilight.
eve•ning (EEV ning) *noun, plural* **evenings.**

explain To give a reason for. *Explain* why you were late.
▲ **Synonyms:** make clear, say.
ex•plain (ek SPLAYN) *verb,* **explained, explaining.**

explore To look around a place and discover new things. Nancy and Robert couldn't wait to *explore* their new neighborhood.
▲ **Synonym:** search.
ex•plore (ek SPLOR) *verb,* **explored, exploring.**

extinct No longer existing. The dodo bird became *extinct* because people hunted it.
ex•tinct (ek STINGKT) *adjective;* **extinction** *noun.*

Ff

fact Something that is real or true. It is a *fact* that there are 50 states in the United States.
▲ **Synonym:** truth.
fact (FAKT) *noun, plural* **facts.**

favorite Liked best. I always wear my *favorite* cap.
▲ **Synonym:** preferred. **fa•vor•ite** (FAY vuhr iht) *adjective.*

Fernando (fur NAN doh)

field 1. An area of land where some games are played. Football is played on a football *field.* **2.** An area of land that has no trees, used for growing grass or food. We planted corn in this *field.*
▲ **Synonym:** grass. **field** (FEELD) *noun, plural* **fields.**

fierce Wild and dangerous. A hungry lion is *fierce.*
▲ **Synonyms:** ferocious, savage. **fierce** (FIHRS) *adjective,* **fiercer, fiercest.**

forest A large area of land covered by trees and plants. They camped in the *forest.*
▲ **Synonym:** woods. **for•est** (FOR ist) *noun; plural* **forests.**

forever 1. For all time; without ever coming to an end. Things cannot stay the same *forever.* **2.** Always; on and on. That grouch is *forever* complaining.
for•ev•er (for EV uhr) *adverb.*

fossil What is left of an animal or plant that lived a long time ago. Fossils are found in rocks, earth, or clay. The bones and footprints of dinosaurs are *fossils.*
▲ **Synonyms:** relic, remains **fos•sil** (FOS uhl) *noun, plural* **fossils.**

fresh Newly made, done, or gathered. We ate *fresh* tomatoes from June's garden.
▲ **Synonyms:** sweet, new, unused. **fresh** (FRESH) *adjective,* **fresher, freshest.**

Gg

glue 1. A material used for sticking things together. I used *glue* to stick the magazine pictures on the paper. *Noun.* **2.** To stick things together with glue. Please *glue* the pieces of the vase together. *Verb.*

    glue (GLOO) *noun, plural* **glues;** *verb,* **glued, gluing.**

goalie The player who defends the goal in soccer, hockey, and some other games. The *goalie* stopped the puck.

    goal•ie (GOHL ee) *noun, plural* **goalies.**

golden 1. Made of or containing gold. My mother has a pair of *golden* earrings. **2.** Having the color or shine of gold; bright or shining. The field of *golden* wheat swayed in the wind.

    gol•den (GOHL duhn) *adjective.*

guess 1. To form an opinion without sure knowledge. Did you *guess* how much that would cost? *Verb.* **2.** An opinion formed without enough information. My *guess* is that the trip will take four hours. *Noun*

    guess (GES) *verb,* **guessed, guessing;** *noun, plural* **guesses.**

Hh

halftime A rest period in the middle of some games. The players had a chance to cool off at *halftime*.

    half•time (HAF tīm) *noun, plural* **halftimes.**

401

hammock A swinging bed made from a long piece of canvas or netting. She fell asleep in the *hammock.*

> **ham•mock** (HAM uhk) *noun, plural* **hammocks.**

harm An injury. She put the baby where he would be safe from *harm. Noun.*

> ▲ **Synonyms:** hurt, wrong, **harm** (HAHRM) *noun, plural* **harms;** *verb,* **harmed, harming.**

heavy Hard to lift or move. The bag of groceries was too *heavy* for Derek to lift.

> ▲ **Synonyms:** hefty, weighty. **heav•y** (HEV ee) *adjective,* **heavier, heaviest.**

hibernate To spend the winter sleeping. Some bears, woodchucks, frogs, and snakes *hibernate* all winter.

> **hi•ber•nate** (HĪ buhr nayt) *verb,* **hibernated, hibernating;** *noun,* **hibernation.**

hidden Past participle of **hide.** To put yourself or something else in a place where it cannot be seen. My cat likes to stay *hidden* under my bed.

> ▲ **Synonym:** unseen. **hide** (HĪD) *verb,* **hid, hidden** (HIHD uhn) or **hid, hiding.**

hunt 1. To look hard to find something or someone. I will *hunt* all over my room until I find my watch. *Verb.* 2. A search to try to find something or someone. We went on a *hunt* through all the stores to find the toy he wanted. *Noun.*

> **hunt** (HUNT) *verb,* **hunted, hunting;** *noun, plural* **hunts.**

Ii

ichthyosaur Any of an extinct group of porpoise-like marine reptiles. **ich•thy•o•saur** (IHK thee oh sor) *noun.*

iguanodon (ih GWAH nuh don)

insect Any of a large group of small animals without a backbone. Insects have a body divided into three parts, with three pairs of legs and usually two pairs of wings. Flies, ants, grasshoppers, and beetles are *insects.*
    in•sect (IN sekt) *noun, plural* **insects.**

intercept To stop or take something on its way from one person or place to another. I tried to pass the ball to a teammate, but a player on the other team *intercepted* it.
    in•ter•cept (IHN tuhr sept) *verb,* **intercepted, intercepting.**

Ll

La Brea (lah BRAY uh)

layer One thickness of something. A *layer* of dust covered the table. **lay•er** (LAY uhr) *noun, plural* **layers.**

lily A large flower shaped like a trumpet. **lil•y** (LIHL ee) *noun, plural* **lilies.**

Mm

machine A thing invented to do a particular job. Airplanes are *machines* that fly.
    ▲ **Synonyms:** device, mechanism. **ma•chine** (muh SHEEN) *noun, plural* **machines.**

403

magazine A printed collection of stories, articles, and pictures usually bound in a paper cover. I read that article about fossils in a nature *magazine*.
> **mag•a•zine** (MAG uh zeen) *noun, plural* **magazines.**

marigold A garden plant that bears yellow, orange, or red flowers in the summer.
> **mar•i•gold** (MAR ih gohld) *noun, plural* **marigolds.**

marvel **1.** A wonderful or amazing thing. Space travel is one of the *marvels* of modern science. *Noun.* **2.** To feel wonder and astonishment. We *marveled* at the acrobat's skill. *Verb.*
> **mar•vel** (MAHR vuhl) *noun, plural* **marvels;** *verb,* **marveled, marveling.**

medusa A jellyfish.
> **me•du•sa** (muh DOO suh) *noun, plural* **medusas** or **medusae.**

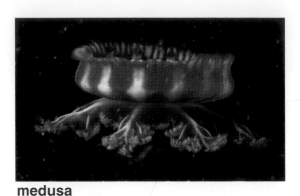
medusa

membrane A thin, flexible layer of skin or tissue that lines parts of the body. The skin that connects a bat's wing bones to its body is called a *membrane*.
> **mem•brane** (MEM brayn) *noun, plural* **membranes.**

middle A place halfway between two points or sides. Noon is in the *middle* of the day.
> ▲ **Synonym:** center.
> **mid•dle** (MIHD uhl) *noun, plural* **middles.**

midnight Twelve o'clock at night; the middle of the night. Cinderella's coach turned into a pumpkin at *midnight*.
> **mid•night** (MIHD nīt) *noun.*

miller A person who owns or operates a mill, especially one for grinding grain. The *miller* sold the wheat to the baker.
mill•er (MIHL uhr) *noun, plural* **millers.**

million 1. One thousand times one thousand; 1,000,000. *Noun.* **2.** Having a very large number. It looks like a *million* stars in the sky. *Adjective.*
mil•lion (MIHL yuhn) *noun, plural* **millions;** *adjective.*

mine A large area dug out in or under the ground. Coal and gold are dug out of *mines.*
mine (MĪN) *noun, plural* **mines.**

mosquito A small insect with two wings. The female gives a sting or bite that itches. There were hundreds of *mosquitoes* near the swamp.
mos•qui•to (muh SKEE toh) *noun, plural* **mosquitoes** or **mosquitos.**

museum A building where pieces of art, science displays, or objects from history are kept for people to see. I saw one of George Washington's hats at the history *museum.*
mu•se•um (myoo ZEE uhm) *noun, plural* **museums.**

music A beautiful combination of sounds. When you sing or play an instrument, you are making *music.*
mu•sic (MYOO zihk) *noun.*

musician A person who is skilled in playing a musical instrument, writing music, or singing. The *musician* prepared to play for the audience.
mu•si•cian (myoo ZIHSH uhn) *noun, plural* **musicians.**

405

mussel An animal that looks like a clam. Saltwater *mussels* have bluish-black shells.
▲ Another word that sounds like this is *muscle*. **mus•sel** (MUS uhl) *noun, plural* **mussels.**

Nn

nature All things in the world that are not made by people. Plants, animals, mountains, and oceans are all part of *nature*. **na•ture** (NAY chuhr) *noun.*

nervous **1.** Not able to relax. Loud noises make me *nervous*. **2.** Fearful or timid. I am very *nervous* about taking the test.
▲ Synonym: anxious. **nerv•ous** (NUR vuhs) *adjective.*

noisy Making harsh or loud sounds. It is *noisy* at the airport.
▲ Synonym: loud. **nois•y** (NOY zee) *adjective,* **noisier, noisiest.**

Oo

object Anything that can be seen and touched. Is that large, round *object* an orange?
▲ Synonym: thing. **ob•ject** (OB jihkt) *noun, plural* **objects.**

offer To present for someone to take or refuse. Mom *offered* to pick us up if it gets dark before the game ends.
▲ Synonym: volunteer, give. **of•fer** (AHF uhr) *verb,* **offered, offering.**

office A place where people work. The principal's *office* is at the end of the hall.
▲ Synonym: workplace. **of•fice** (AHF ihs) *noun, plural* **offices.**

out-of-bounds In sports, outside the area of play allowed. I kicked the ball *out-of-bounds,* so the other team was given the ball.
   out•of•bounds (OWT uv BOWNDZ) *adverb, adjective.*

Pp

package A thing or group of things that are packed in a box, wrapped up, or tied in a bundle. We sent a *package* of treats to my sister at camp.
   ▲ **Synonyms:** bundle, parcel. **pack•age** (PAK ihj) *noun, plural* **packages.**

Parthenon (PAHR thuh nahn)

piece A part that has been broken, cut, or torn from something. There are *pieces* of broken glass on the floor.
   piece (PEES) *noun, plural* **pieces.**

practice To do something over and over to gain skill. I *practice* playing guitar every day.
   prac•tice (PRAK tihs) *verb,* **practiced, practicing.**

preserve To keep from being damaged, decayed, or lost; protect. You can *preserve* the wood of the table by waxing it.
   pre•serve (prih ZURV) *verb,* **preserved, preserving.**

princess The daughter of a king or queen; a female member of a royal family other than a queen; the wife of a prince. The people of the kingdom bowed to the *princess.*
   prin•cess (PRIHN sihs *or* PRIHN ses) *noun, plural* **princesses.**

principal The person who is the head of a school. The *principal* gave a speech.
▲ Another word that sounds like this is *principle*. **prin•ci•pal** (PRIHN suh puhl) *noun, plural* **principals.**

problem Anything that causes trouble and must be dealt with. A barking dog can be a *problem*. **prob•lem** (PRAHB luhm) *noun, plural* **problems.**

prowl To move or roam quietly or secretly. The tiger *prowled* through the forest. **prowl** (PROWL) *verb,* **prowled, prowling.**

Rr

reptile One of a class of cold-blooded animals with a backbone and dry, scaly skin. Lizards are *reptiles*. **rep•tile** (REP tīl) *noun, plural* **reptiles.**

restaurant A place where food is prepared and served. We ate at the *restaurant*. **res•tau•rant** (RES tuh ruhnt or RES tuh rahnt) *noun, plural* **restaurants.**

roof The top part of a building. There was a leak in the *roof*. **roof** (ROOF *or* RŬF) *noun, plural* **roofs.**

Ss

save 1. To keep from harm; to make safe. The cat *saved* her kittens from the fire. 2. To set aside for future use. I will *save* some cookies to eat later. **save** (SAYV) *verb,* **saved, saving.**

scare To make afraid. Loud noises always *scare* the puppy.
▲ **Synonyms:** alarm, frighten. **scare** (SKAIR) *verb,* **scared, scaring.**

scary Causing alarm or fear; frightening. Your monster costume is very *scary*.
scar•y (SKAIR ee) *adjective,* **scarier, scariest.**

score 1. To get a point or points in a game or on a test. The baseball team *scored* five runs in one inning. *Verb.* **2.** The points gotten in a game or on a test. The final *score* was 5 to 4. *Noun.*
▲ **Synonym:** tally. **score** (SKOR) *verb,* **scored, scoring;** *noun, plural* **scores.**

sea anemone A sea animal shaped like a tube that attaches itself to rocks and to other objects.
sea a•nem•o•ne (SEE uh NEM uh nee) *noun, plural* **sea anemones.**

seaweed Any plant or plants that grows in the sea, especially certain kinds of algae.
sea•weed (SEE weed) *noun.*

señor Sir; mister. Spanish form of respectful or polite address for a man. **se•ñor** (sen YOR)

señora Mistress; madam. Spanish form of respectful or polite address for a woman. **se•ño•ra** (sen YOR uh)

servant A person hired to work for the comfort or protection of others. The *servant* brought in their dinner.
serv•ant (SUR vuhnt) *noun, plural* **servants.**

several More than two, but not many. We saw *several* of our friends at the parade.
▲ **Synonym:** various.
  sev•er•al (SEV uhr ul *or* SEV ruhl) *adjective; noun.*

shoulder The part on either side of the body from the neck to where the arm joins. I carry the sack over my *shoulder*.
  shoul•der (SHOHL duhr) *noun, plural* **shoulders.**

skeleton A framework that supports and protects the body. Birds, fish, and humans have *skeletons* made of bones.
  skel•e•ton (SKEL uh tuhn) *noun, plural* **skeletons.**

slip To slide and fall down. Be careful not to *slip* on the wet floor.
▲ **Synonyms:** slide, skid.
  slip (SLIHP) *verb,* **slipped, slipping.**

soil The top part of the ground in which plants grow. There is sandy *soil* near the coast.
▲ **Synonyms:** dirt, earth.
  soil (SOYL) *noun, plural* **soils.**

station A place of business where something specific is done. We get gas for a car at a gas *station*. Police officers work in a police *station*.
▲ **Synonym:** precinct.
  sta•tion (STAY shuhn) *noun, plural* **stations.**

stepmother A woman who has married a person's father after the death or divorce of the natural mother. Dan's *stepmother* came to his school play.
  step•moth•er (STEP muthh uhr) *noun, plural* **stepmothers.**

storyteller A person who tells or writes stories.

> **sto•ry•tell•er** (STOR ee tel uhr) *noun, plural* **storytellers.**

stretch To spread out to full length. The lazy cat *stretched* and then went back to sleep.
▲ **Synonym:** extend. **stretch** (STRECH) *verb,* **stretched, stretching.**

study To try to learn by reading, thinking about, or looking; examine closely. A detective *studies* clues carefully.

> **stud•y** (STUD ee) *verb,* **studied, studying.**

sway To move back and forth. The tree branches *swayed.*
▲ **Synonyms:** swing, wave, lean. **sway** (SWAY) *verb,* **swayed, swaying.**

swift Moving or able to move very quickly. The rider had a *swift* horse.
▲ **Synonyms:** speedy, fast. **swift** (SWIHFT) *adjective,* **swifter, swiftest.**

swivel chair A chair with a seat that spins. She spun around on the *swivel chair.*

> **swi•vel chair** (SWIHV uhl chair) *noun, plural* **swivel chairs.**

Tt

teenager A person who is between the ages of thirteen and nineteen.

> **teen•a•ger** (TEEN ay juhr) *noun, plural* **teenagers.**

termite An insect that eats wood, paper, and other materials. The *termites* ate through the floor of the old house.

> **ter•mite** (TUR mīt) *noun, plural* **termites.**

therapy Treatment for a disability, injury, psychological problem, or illness. He needed physical *therapy* to help heal his broken leg.
 ther•a•py (THER uh pee) *noun, plural* **therapies.**

third Next after the second one. We had seats in the *third* row of the theater.
 third (THURD) *adjective.*

throne **1.** The chair that a king or queen sits on during ceremonies and other special occasions. **2.** The power or authority of a king or queen.
 throne (THROHN) *noun, plural* **thrones.**

throw To send something through the air. *Throw* the ball to the dog, and she will bring it back to you.
 ▲ **Synonyms:** toss, fling, pitch.
 throw (THROH) *verb,* **threw, thrown, throwing.**

thumbtack A tack with a flat, round head that can be pressed into a wall or board with the thumb. Notices are often pinned to bulletin boards with *thumbtacks.*
 thumb•tack (THUM tak) *noun, plural* **thumbtacks.**

ton A measure of weight equal to 2,000 pounds in the United States and Canada, and 2,240 pounds in Great Britain.
 ton (tun) *noun, plural* **tons.**

tooth One of the hard, white, bony parts in the mouth used for biting and chewing. I got a filling in my front *tooth.*
>**tooth** (TOOTH) *noun,* *plural* **teeth.**

touch To put your hand on or against something. If you *touch* the stove, you will get burned.
>▲ **Synonym:** feel.
>**touch** (TUCH) *verb,* **touched, touching.**

trilobite An extinct sea animal that lived hundreds of millions of years ago.
>**tri•lo•bite** (TRĪ loh bīt) *noun,* *plural* **trilobites.**

Uu

upstairs **1.** On or to a higher floor. My bedroom is *upstairs.* *Adverb.* **2.** On an upper floor. The *upstairs* bathroom was just cleaned. *Adjective.*
>**up•stairs** (UP stairz) *adverb;* *adjective.*

Vv

vacation A period of rest or freedom. Summer *vacation* begins next week.
>**va•ca•tion** (vay KAY shuhn) *noun, plural* **vacations.**

village A small town. The streets of the *village* were paved with stones.
>▲ **Synonym:** community.
>**vil•lage** (VIHL ihj) *noun, plural* **villages.**

voice The sound you make through your mouth. You use your *voice* when you sing.
>**voice** (VOYS) *noun, plural* **voices.**

Ww

warn alert; To tell about something before it happens.
>**warn** (WORN) *verb,* **warned, warning.**

413

waterfall A natural stream of water falling from a high place. We had a picnic by the *waterfall.* **wa•ter•fall** (WAH tuhr fawl) *noun, plural* **waterfalls.**

wheelchair A chair on wheels that is used by someone who cannot walk to get from one place to another. He needed a *wheelchair* until his leg healed. **wheel•chair** (HWEEL chair *or* WEEL chair) *noun, plural* **wheelchairs.**

whistle 1. To make a sound by pushing air out through your lips or teeth. My dog comes when I *whistle. Verb.* **2.** Something you blow into that makes a whistling sound. The police officer blew his *whistle. Noun.* **whis•tle** (HWIS uhl *or* WIS uhl) *verb,* **whistled, whistling;** *noun, plural* **whistles.**

wipe To clean or dry by rubbing. ▲**Synonym:** clean. **wipe** (WĪP) *verb,* **wiped, wiping.**

wonder 1. To want to know or learn; be curious about. I *wonder* why the sky is blue. *Verb.* **2.** A surprising or impressive thing. *Noun.* **won•der** (WUN duhr) *verb,* **wondered, wondering;** *noun, plural* **wonders.**

world Place where all things live. **world** (WURLD) *noun, plural* **worlds.**

wrap To cover something by putting something else around it. We will *wrap* the package. **wrap** (RAP) *verb,* **wrapped, wrapping.**

Xx

xiphactinus (zee FAK tī nus)

Zz

zinnia A garden flower. **zin•ni•a** (ZIHN nee uh) *noun, plural* **zinnias.**

ACKNOWLEDGMENTS

The publisher gratefully acknowledges permission to reprint the following copyrighted material:

"Charlie Anderson" by Barbara Abercrombie, illustrated by Mark Graham. Text copyright © 1990 by Barbara Abercrombie. Illustrations copyright © 1990 by Mark Graham. Reprinted with permission of Margaret K. McElderry Books, Simon & Schuster Children's Publishing Division.

"Fernando's Gift" by Douglas Keister. Copyright © 1995 by Douglas Keister. Reprinted by permission of Sierra Club Books For Children.

"Fossils Tell of Long Ago" by Aliki. Copyright © 1972, 1990 by Aliki Brandenberg. Used by permission of HarperCollins Publishers.

"Neighbors" by Marchette Chute from RHYMES ABOUT US. by Marchette Chute. Published 1974 by E.P. Dutton. Reprinted with permission of Elizabeth Hauser.

"Officer Buckle and Gloria" by Peggy Rathmann. Copyright ©, Peggy Rathmann, 1995. Published by arrangement with Penguin Putnam Books for Young Readers, a division of Penguin Putnam Inc.

"Our Soccer League" from OUR SOCCER LEAGUE by Chuck Solomon. Text copyright © 1988 by Chuck Solomon. Reprinted by arrangement with Random House Children's Books, a division of Random House, Inc.

"Princess Pooh" is the entire text from PRINCESS POOH by Kathleen M. Muldoon with illustrations by Linda Shute. Text copyright © 1989 by Kathleen M. Muldoon. Illustrations copyright © 1989 by Linda Shute. Originally published in hardcover by Albert Whitman & Company. All rights reserved. Used with permission.

"River Winding" from RIVER WINDING by Charlotte Zolotow. Copyright © 1970 by Charlotte Zolotow. Reprinted by permission of Scott Treimel New York.

"Swimmy" from SWIMMY by Leo Lionni. Copyright © 1963 by Leo Lionni. Copyright renewed 1991 by Leo Lionni. Reprinted by arrangement with Random House Children's Books, a division of Random House, Inc.

"To Catch a Fish" by Eloise Greenfield from UNDER THE SUNDAY TREE. Text copyright © 1988 by Eloise Greenfield. Paintings copyright © 1988 by Amos Ferguson. Reprinted by permission of HarperTrophy, a division of HarperCollins Publishers.

"Tomás and the Library Lady" by Pat Mora. Text copyright © 1977 by Pat Mora. Illustrations copyright © 1997 by Raul Colón. Reprinted by permission of Alfred A. Knopf.

"The Wednesday Surprise" from THE WEDNESDAY SURPRISE by Eve Bunting with illustrations by Donald Carrick. Text copyright © 1989 by Eve Bunting. Illustrations copyright © 1989 by Donald Carrick. Reprinted by permission of Clarion Books, a Houghton Mifflin Co. imprint.

"What Is It?" by Eve Merriam from HIGGLE WIGGLE (MORROW JR BOOKS). Text copyright © 1994 by the Estate of Eve Merriam by Marian Reiner, Literary Executor. Used by permission of Marian Reiner.

"Which?" from CRICKETY CRICKET! THE BEST LOVED POEMS OF JAMES S. TIPPETT. Text copyright © 1933, copyright renewed © 1973 by Martha K. Tippett. Illustrations copyright © 1973 by Mary Chalmers. Reprinted by permission of HarperCollins Publishers.

"Zipping, Zapping, Zooming Bats" by Ann Earle. Text copyright © 1995 by Ann Earle. Illustrations copyright © 1995 by Henry Cole. Reprinted by permission of HarperCollins Children's Books, a division of HarperCollins Publishers.

Illustration

Matt Straub, 12–13; Leonor Glynn, 42; Claude Martinot, 43; Kuenhee Lee, 44–45; Myron Grossman, 67; Annette Cable, 68–69; Cecily Lang, 70–87; Claude Martinot, 91; Tim Raglin, 92–93; Claude Martinot, 115; Melinda Levine, 130–131; Mary GrandPre, 132–145; Julia Gorton, 149; Tom Barrett, 150–151; Myron Grossman, 179; Joe Cepeda, 180–181; Leonor Glynn, 210; Julia Gorton, 211; Suling Wang, 212–213; Vilma Ortiz–Dillon, 234; Myron Grossman, 235; Anne Lunsford, 282–283; Myron Grossman, 309; Jerry Smath, 250–251; Julia Gorton, 281; Abby Carter, 310–311;

Claude Martinot, 339; Carol Inouye, 340–341; Claude Martinot, 361; Robert Crawford, 10–11; Taylor Bruce, 126–127; Russ Willms, 128–129; Marina Thompson, 248–249; Sonja Lamut, 372–373; Tom Leonard, 116–117; Myron Grossman, 125, 371; Michael Welch, 236–237; Claude Martinot, 245; Alexandra Wallner, 362–363; John Carozza, 410; Holly Jones, 394, 403; Miles Parnell, 398, 407, 412.

Photography

4: b. Douglas Keister; 5: b. Merline Tuttle/Photo Researchers; 7: b, John Cancalosis/Peter Arnold; 9: b. David Muench/Corbis; 41: r. Renee Lynn/Photo Researchers/l. Renee Lynn/Photo Researchers/Dough Plummer/Photonica; 42: b.r. Renee Lynn/Photo Researchers; 65: b. Andrea Pistolesi/The Image Bank; 70: b.r. Courtesy of Cecily Lang Studio/t.l. Courtesy of Diane Hoyt–Goldsmith; 75: t. Roy Morsch/The Stock Market/b. Brown Brothers; 77: r. Wernher Kruten/Liaison International/l. Chad Ehlers/Tony Stone Images; 79: b. Zigy Kalunzy/Tony Stone Images; 81: Merlin D. Tuttle/Bat Conservation International; 83: t. Wesley Hitt/Liaison International/b. Superstock; 84: Howard Grey/Tony Stone Images; 85: Robert Landau/Westlight; 87: t.r. Hiroyuki Matsumoto/Tony Stone Images/b.r. Marc Biggins/Liaison International/b.l. Tom Bean/Tony Stone/t.l. Superstock; 89: b. Merlin D. Tuttle/Bat Conservation International/t. Wesley Hitt/Liaison International; 94: t.l. Courtesy of HarperCollins Publishers; 113: b. T. Sawada/Photonica; 114: m.l. Merlin D. Tuttle/Bat Conservation International/t.r. Merlin D. Tuttle/Bat Conservation International/t.l. Merlin D. Tuttle/Bat Conservation International/b.r. Stephen Dalton/Photo Researchers; 122: t. Merlin D. Tuttle/Photo Researchers/m. Joe Mcdonald/Animals Animals/b. Merlin Tuttle/Bat Conservation International; 123: b. PhotoDisc; 132: Courtesy of the artist; 176-177: David Madison/Tony Stone Images; 214: T. Carolina Ambida. 233: b. Jeffrey Sylvester/FPG International; 242: t.l. PhotoDisc/b.r. Howard Grey/Tony Stone Images/m.l. PhotoDisc; 244: l. PhotoDisc/r. Howard Grey/Tony Stone Images; 252: t. Courtesy of Penguin Putnam Inc.; 279: m.r. Jonathan Nourok/Photo Edit/b. Tom Nebbia/Corbis-Bettman/m.c. David Young-Wolff/Photo Edit/m.l. Spencer Grant/Photo Edit; 284: t.l. Courtesy Random House/b.r. Courtesy of Raul Colon/t.l. Courtesy Alfred A. Knopf Inc.; 306-307: Tony Freeman/Photo Edit; 337: b. Jim Cummins/FPG International/m.r. PhotoDisc; 360: t. PhotoDisc/b. PhotoDisc; 368: m. Kit Latham/FPG.

Reading for Information
All photographs are by Macmillan/McGraw-Hill (MMH); Michael Groen for MMH; Ken Karp for MMH; and Chuck Solomon for MMH, except as noted below.

Table of Contents, pp. 374–375
Chess pieces, tl, Wides + Hall/FPG; Earth, mcl, M. Burns/Picture Perfect; CD's, mcl, Michael Simpson/FPG; Newspapers, bl, Craig Orsini/Index Stock/PictureQuest; Clock, tc, Steve McAlister/The Image Bank; Kids circle, bc, Daniel Pangbourne Media/FPG; Pencils, tr, W. Cody/Corbis; Starfish, tc, Darryl Torckler/Stone; Keys, cr, Randy Faris/Corbis; Cells, br, Spike Walker/Stone; Stamps, tr, Michael W. Thomas/Focus Group/PictureQuest; Books, cr, Siede Preis/PhotoDisc; Sunflower, cr, Jeff LePore/Natural Selection; Mouse, br, Andrew Hall/Stone; Apples, tr, Siede Preis/PhotoDisc; Watermelons, br, Neil Beer/PhotoDisc; Butterfly, br, Stockbyte

377: t.r. George Godfrey/Earth Scenes/b.r. Leonard Lee Rue/Stock Boston; 378-379: bkgd. Tom Walker/Stock Boston; 380: m.l. George Bernard/Animals Animals/m.r. M. MC. Chamberlain/DRK Photo/b.l. David Baron/Animals Animals; 380-381 bkgd. William Johnson/Stock Boston; 381: t.l. Fritz Polking/Dembinsky Photo Assoc./b.l. E. R. Dergginger/Dembinsky Photo Assoc.; 390: l. PhotoDisc; 392: Ron Chapple/FPG International; 393: Jose Azel/Aurora/PNI; 395: David Stockein/The Stock Market; 396: Mark A. Johnson/The Stock Market; 397: Tom Dean/The Stock Market; 398: Wayne Levin/FPG International; 400: Eric Meola/The Image Bank; 401: David Brooks/The Stock Market; 402: Michel Renaudeau/Liaison; 405: Don Perdue/Liaison; 406: Richard H. Johnston/FPG International; 408: Rick Rusing/Tony Stone Images; 409: Darryl Torchker/Tony Stone Images; 411: Hank de Lespinasse/Image Bank; 412: Adam Woolfitt/Woodfin Camp, Inc.